Religion
and
Social Conflicts

OTTO MADURO

Religion
and
Social Conflicts

Translated from the Spanish by
Robert R. Barr

ORBIS BOOKS
Maryknoll, New York 10545

The Catholic Foreign Mission Society of America (Maryknoll) recruits and trains people for overseas missionary service. Through Orbis Books Maryknoll aims to foster the international dialogue that is essential to mission. The books published, however, reflect the opinions of their authors and are not meant to represent the official position of the society.

First published as *Religión y lucha de clases* by Editorial Ateneo de Caracas, Apdo. 662, Caracas, Venezuela, copyright © 1979 by Otto Maduro; also published as *Religion y conflicto social* by the Centro de Reflexión Teológica, A.C., Apdo. postal 19-213, Colonia Mixcoac, 03910 México, D.F., Mexico

English translation copyright © 1982 by Orbis Books, Maryknoll, NY 10545

Manufactured in the United States of America

Manuscript Editor: William E. Jerman

Library of Congress Cataloging in Publication Data
Maduro, Otto, 1945–
    Religion and social conflicts.

    Translation of: Religion y lucha de clases.
    Bibliography: p.
    1. Religion and sociology. 2. Sociology, Christian. 3. Sociology, Christian—Latin America. 4. Social change. I. Title.
BL60.M2813   306'.6'098   82-3439
ISBN 0-88344-428-3 (pbk.)   AACR2

CONTENTS

ACKNOWLEDGMENTS

This book is part of the fruit of six years of research, 1971 to 1977, at the Catholic University of Louvain, in Belgium, and a seventh year, 1977 to 1978, at the University of the Andes, in Venezuela. I wish to express my thanks to the administration of the University of the Andes, where I have been working since 1969, for the grant that afforded me the time and calm I needed to carry out my research in Louvain.

At the Catholic University of Louvain, I owe a special debt of gratitude to—once again—Dr. François Houtart, director of the Center for Socio-Religious Research (CRSR), for his instruction (direct and indirect), as well as for his continual inspiration in my studies and reflections; likewise to Professor André Berten, of the Higher Institute of Philosophy, for the intellectual and human sustenance he has offered me since the very first steps in my research; to Professors Jean Remy, Jean-Pierre Hiernaux, and Georges Liénard, of the Center for Urban and Rural Sociology (CSUR), for what I have been able to learn from their lectures and writings.

Outside Louvain my appreciation goes to Jacques Verscheure (France), Gustavo Guizzardi (Italy), and Theo Steeman (United States), for their invitations to give seminars in the institutions with which they are affiliated. Those opportunities forced me to deepen, systematize, and explain the ideas that I am now setting forth.

Finally, as is the custom (and it is still a valid one), I claim exclusive responsibility for any shortcomings or errors in form or content in this book.

FOREWORD TO THE
ENGLISH TRANSLATION

Otto Maduro has produced a book written for Latin American readers that also provides for North Americans a scholarly interpretation of what is happening in Latin America today. Having studied at Louvain, he has learned the tools of sociological analysis customarily used in Europe and North America for understanding how social systems work, and he has taken these seriously. They have enabled him to understand quite clearly what has transpired between the colonizers and the colonized historically in Latin America. He recognizes, however, that the situation could look quite different from other points of view. With that in mind he has formally chosen to re-examine the same process through the theoretical models of Marxism to see what the observation of class conflict reveals.

For those who wonder how a Marxist analysis can be consistently and informatively applied to the Latin American situation and still not treat the reality of Christianity as purely epiphenomenal, this book is a splendid assignment. One may feel, as I did, that the analysis pushes too hard in a few places, but the final resolution is a satisfying exercise and one that surely needs to be taken on by any number of sociologists of religion, other scholars, and people in general committed to a more adequate critical social analysis prior to effective action for social change in a social justice perspective.

Through this excellent translation we are allowed to observe while Maduro engages his fellow Latin Americans in a critical analysis of the Church in society. He is inviting Latin Americans to engage in an exercise of model-rejecting and model-using. He suggests that the function of religion is sufficiently unique in different countries to need an intensive study in context. Catholicism, he notes, does not play the same role in Vietnam, Northern Ireland, and Algeria as it does in Latin America. He claims that without knowledge of the historical journey of a religion in a given environmental setting one cannot generalize from any theory as to what will happen next. He uses Marxist theory as a guide to questions and theses for the examination of role relations within the religious system between the ruling and the ruled and between the religious system, the state, and the economy on the basis of a changing division of authority. He shows that one can come to clear insights about the form that the religious culture takes, the content of the affirmed worldview, and the effect this has on the function of religion in a society. He has little to say in favor of anthropological studies that locate the religious system within the functioning societal structure on the assumption that this constitutes a moving equilibrium. He demonstrates rather the changing role of religion depending on the worldview it celebrates and the class links it has.

His perspective is of special value to North Americans today because it provides an analysis of the perceived effects of Western European and North American presence in Latin America from the point of view of a scholar whose own experience, as a native of Venezuela, is within the Latin American setting. His critical analysis is intended to enlighten Latin Americans about the relationship between religion and social change in their own cultures. Learning by observing the interactions of others is a valuable experience for First World peoples like us.

Using the Marxist theory of religion, Maduro pushes the analysis of religion as a societal product as far as he can, secure in his own understanding that this does not exhaust the reality of religion. He concludes that in societies that have historically shared a common religious worldview, religion can be an effective intervening variable in a class struggle for greater autonomy from oppression, if the religion role-players work together with the members of the oppressed classes to achieve their autonomy from the cultural and psychic control embedded in a worldview fashioned for them by the controlling classes. He indicates that the potential for harmony embodied in a new worldview must await its transcendent harmonious promise at some time after justice is done. His abiding faith, reflected in the final resolution of his thesis, is inspiring and credible.

Sister Marie Augusta Neal, SND
Emmanuel College, Boston

FOREWORD:

WHAT IS RELIGION GOOD FOR WITHIN CLASS STRUGGLES?

Otto Maduro approaches his subject in a most novel way. The left has long since issued its condemnation of religion. The right, by contrast, has spent the last decade revising some of its traditional certitudes. There used to be a kind of agreement on both sides that religion is the solid stanchion of the established order, good for nothing but the ideology of the dominating class. But today, in Latin America, this class is itself beginning to denounce the church as "subversive and revolutionary"—witness the following eloquent testimonials from the august pens of the Mexican Anticommunist Federation (*Federación Mexicana Anticomunista,* FEMACO), the Latin American Anticommunist Confederation (*Confederación Anticomunista Latinoamericana,* CAL), Nelson A. Rockefeller, and the Rand Corporation, in a study for the United States Department of State.

Document of the FEMACO

WHEREAS the activity deployed by infiltrators of the hierarchy of the Catholic clergy constitutes the greatest danger of communism in Latin America; and

WHEREAS said danger is partly owing, on the one hand, to the ancestral piety of our people and, on the other, to the form in which such clergy cloak their subversive activities in priestly vestments, utilizing them as authorization to serve communism with impunity; and

WHEREAS the activity of progressive clergymen, who have entered into a conspiracy with communism to overthrow loyal governments, is become more and more virulent, constituting a hopeless pitfall for the social and political stability of Latin American states, as witness the occurrences of Riobamba,[1] or the strategies mapped by CELAM [Conferencia Episcopal Latinoamericana, Latin American Episcopal Conference] in order to attain its objectives, beginning with Medellín, in Colombia;[2] and

WHEREAS the perversity and unscrupulousness of those who have infiltrated the hierarchy of the Catholic clergy in Latin America know

no limits, as is abundantly demonstrated by its so-called theology of
liberation, which is simply the class struggle mounted astride the gospel
and interpreting it dialectically, or as evidenced by the publication of
the so-called *Latin American Bible*, which is nothing but an instrument
of Marxist indoctrination;[3] and

WHEREAS the peoples and governments of Latin America have no
practical canonical recourse for curbing these activities, inasmuch as
they are fostered by the upper echelons of the hierarchy, with the atten-
dant reduction to helplessness of governments that might have wished
to have such recourse in order to curb the subversive activities of a
progressive clergy in the service of communism. . . .[4]

So begins the document submitted to the Third Congress of the Latin American Anticommunist Federation meeting in Asunción, Paraguay, in March
1977. This is the tone that prevails in all the documents of that congress,
which make the church the center of their anticommunist attention.

To these persons, obsessed as they are with the struggle against social
change in Latin America, it seems evident that the religion that predominates
on our continent has become a dangerous force of subversion in today's class
struggles. The same congress included the following in its resolutions.

Document of the CAL

[We] denounce the strategy of communist infiltration, in full bloom
within the church. It comprises tactical plans for the subversion of various activities of this church, such as pastoral letters, episcopal documents, preaching, catechetical programs, seminaries, and Catholic
high schools and universities.

The document proposes certain tasks:

Creation by the CAL of permanent propaganda organizations to warn
the Christian faithful in Latin America of Marxist infiltration in their
churches; . . . creation of a central planning office for the distribution
of propaganda materials geared to establishing, bolstering, and orientating a sense of struggle against communist infiltration in the church
of Latin America; . . . solicitation of anticommunist governments of
Latin America to the effect that they use the appropriate diplomatic
channels to keep the Holy See permanently informed of Marxist-
Leninist activities infiltrating the Catholic hierarchy and clergy of their
respective nations, and that they intercede on behalf of those anti-
Marxist ecclesiastics who are unjustly marginalized from activities for
which they are competent.

The obsession of these "anticommunists" with a defense of their own
privileges may be leading them to distort the role of religion in the struggles

they seek to terminate. But underlying the distortions there would seem to be a measure of truth, which has fairly shaken the life of the church over this past decade (though its roots date from an earlier period), and continues to do so with deepening intensity.

This whole phenomenon evinces the insufficiency, indeed the error, of a theological focus that sees no alternative for religion but to serve as an ideological instrument of the dominant class for the consecration and perpetuation of the existing order. At the same time it calls into question the analyses of Latin America that see the Catholic Church, and Christianity as a whole, constituting, evidently and uniformly, a conservative, reactionary force.

The Rockefeller Report

As early as 1969, Nelson A. Rockefeller took cognizance of this change of the status quo, in his "Report on the Americas," to President Nixon. Nixon, as we know, had dispatched a mission, led by Rockefeller, to our part of the Americas in that year, with the assigned task of composing a report for the orientation of North American political strategy. Rockefeller and his mission paid visits to twenty countries, and more than two thousand leaders in these countries, before filing their August 1969 report—much as the Stevenson mission had done eight years before as a basis for the Alliance for Progress.

The Rockefeller report sees the social significance of the Catholic Church in these terms:

The Cross and the Sword

Although it is not yet widely recognized, the military establishments and the Catholic Church are also among today's forces for social and political change in the other American republics. This is a new role for them. For since the arrival of the Conquistadores more than four hundred years ago, the history of the military and the Catholic Church, working hand in hand with the landowners to provide "stability," has been a legend in the Americas.

Few people realize the extent to which both these institutions are now breaking with their pasts. They are, in fact, moving rapidly to the forefront as forces for social, economic, and political change. In the case of the Church, this is a recognition of a need to be more responsive to the popular will. In the case of the military, it is a reflection of a broadening of opportunities for young men regardless of family background.

The Church

Modern communications and increasing education have brought about a stirring among the people that has had a tremendous impact on the Church, making it a force dedicated to change—revolutionary change if necessary.

Actually, the Church may be somewhat in the same situation as the young—with a profound idealism, but as a result, in some cases, vulnerable to subversive penetration; ready to undertake a revolution if necessary to end injustice, but not clear as to the ultimate nature of the revolution itself or as to the governmental system by which the justice it seeks can be realized.[5]

Here we obviously have a more calm and collected appraisal than the one by the CAL—although both coincide in seeing certain forces in the church as spurring social change on behalf of the oppressed classes. But this type of condensed memorandum has its limitations, which invite a good deal of nuancing in more extensive and specialized studies.

The Rand Study for the State Department

The United States Department of State has concerned itself (and still concerns itself) with just such studies. For instance, we have on hand a study done by the Rand Corporation of California for foreign investigation officials of the State Department, entitled, "Institutional Development in Latin America: Changes in the Catholic Church." This study, carried out by university researchers Luigi Einaudi, Richard Maullin, Alfred Stephan, and Michael Fleet, with the aid of other experts, is "not so much the fruit of a long-term investigation as it is a first effort to reconsider what we have discerned to be a series of very acute and exciting problems. The actual analysis was done during the months from June to September 1969, in Santa Monica, California, amid heated round-table discussion in which each of us began by exaggerating the importance of his own several years of research. We hope our viewpoints will be of service to other researchers in continuing and deepening the treatment of particular problems."[6]

And here is what these experts working for the State Department think:

The Catholic Church in Latin America is in a state of great effervescence—probably more than at any other moment in its history. In part this effervescence reflects the repercussions of world events, including the impact of such movements of major importance as communism, which has called into question the traditional religious roles of the clergy and the laity. But the specific successes and failures of economic modernization and social change in Latin America, along with world events that have had their effect on Catholics in all parts of the world, have combined to yield a set of political and religious responses reflecting the peculiar circumstances of Latin America.

This "effervescence," however, is far from being uniform in makeup. It is not occasioned by currents that flow in only one direction. Rather it reveals, with rare evidence and clarity, the profound class meaning of religion—in spite of the efforts of religious leaders to maintain a peaceful, transclassist universalism. On this continent, with its all-pervading network of opulence and misery, the concrete history of society simply prevents them from doing so.

There is a powerful current against change in the church today—and among those who wish for change there are many different ways of understanding it. Hence, for instance, the fanatical and dogmatic simplism of the CAL document, more appropriate for the Inquisition of old, turns into a series of very meaningful nuances in the hands of the State Department experts. They are more concerned to set forth elements of comprehension for the analysis of the dangers for the empire rather than in engaging in any direct, fanatical crusade. They observe:

> Even among the protagonists of economic and social change there is a basic difference between those who speak of being "in" a revolution and those who speak of "starting" a revolution. For some Catholics, a heightened consciousness among the dispossessed classes (the rural and urban poor) with regard to the need for change, and a higher level of material aspirations within the popular sectors, already constitute revolutionary progress. The mission of the revolutionary, they argue, is to recognize these pressures, and launch them in institutional, democratic, nonviolent channels. For others in the church, however, a revolutionary view demands a drastic restructuring of the prevailing socioeconomic system, whereby the exploitation of man by man can be eradicated. According to this latter view there is still no revolution, and consequently a political strategy that will propose, initiate, and further such revolution becomes necessary.

It is difficult for an outside observer to predict which tendencies will prevail in the church as it attempts to respond to future social occurrences that will be appealing to the very source of its faith—the gospel of Jesus Christ. But this response will be profoundly conditioned by the institutional characteristics of the church then prevailing. Thus the North American analysts rightly observe:

> The limits that the church as an institution can allow to politics actively patronizing violent revolution depend on complex factors of its "institutional weight," which encumber any decisions for coming to grips with the process of change. These factors include the historical conservatism of the church, its institutional interests, questions concerning its finances and/or its relations with the state, and, finally, the impossibility of translating moral abstractions into concrete policies of action without creating tensions, and this could mean the end of a united church of all Catholics.

The church's identification with authority, royalty, tradition, and opposition to change has been in large part the basic criterion for defining political actions in Latin societies. As a consequence, the left, historically, has been anticlerical in Catholic countries. Some of the younger political activists admit the honesty with which some members of the church have come to advocate changes, but there are members of the older generation who tend to be more skeptical. These problems relating to political change also oblige Catholics to ask themselves how they can reconcile revolutionary political activity with the preservation of the church as an institution in a secular world. Why contribute to change if change will probably be hostile?

Naturally, as long as these questions and positions remain confined to the narrow world of the clergy, they are of less concern to the sociologist interested in the possible role of religion in the coming years in Latin America, or for the strategy of the State Department. But this changes when one considers the repercussions on the broad masses of Christians on this continent and their contribution to a rejuvenated social consciousness and a gospel emphasis on justice and a community of brothers and sisters. Hence the Rand study quite rightly observes:

> The ultimate outcome of these reforming attempts will be determined in large part by seculars. The very creation of a consciousness underscores not only the limits of the church's structural opportunities for direct political action, but also the importance of lay response. The impact of the church's changing values will, in the long run, be seen to affect the conduct not only of the clergy, or even only of Catholics, but of all Latin Americans, rich or poor, civil or military.

Ten years later, this impact is still an unknown—even though in many countries the deep commitment of Christians to the dispossessed classes is being accepted, and these classes' consciousness and organization are being quickened, thanks to their religious experience. Today, not only do clergy and bishops denounce torture and misery, but the conflict with some governments and dominant classes has reached a point where several thousand Christians (bishops, priests, nuns, leaders, peasants, laborers, and lay persons linked in any way with Christian associations) have suffered exile, persecution, and even torture and assassination.

CELAM, Puebla, 1979

Which current will prevail is still in the balance. The effort to curb that Christian effort in the class struggles is mighty, within and without the Christian world. Hence the great interest and hopes that were concentrated on the Third General Assembly of the Latin American Episcopal Conference, held in Puebla, Mexico, in February 1979. Hence the presence of twenty-six hundred accredited journalists there. For this was an assembly of bishops who were very painfully aware of the "dangers" besetting the Latin American church along its chosen path—an assembly of bishops some of whom (a minority, doubtless) even shared, in varying degrees, the opinion of the CAL.

Nonetheless, this assembly of some three hundred persons, attempting to respond to the outcry of millions of human beings, came to the following conclusion regarding the ten years just gone by:

> The vast majority of our fellow human beings continue to live in a situation of poverty and even wretchedness that has grown more acute [No. 1135].
> Analyzing this situation more deeply, we discover that this poverty is not a passing phase. Instead it is the product of economic, social, and political situations and structures [No. 30].

Confronted with this state of affairs, the bishops maintain that only one Christian response is possible:

> Hence this reality calls for personal conversion and profound structural changes that will meet the legitimate aspirations of the people for authentic social justice. Such changes either have not taken place, or else they have been too slow in coming in the concrete life of Latin America [No. 30].

And hence the Latin American Bishops' Conference will combine its efforts "with those of people of good will in order to uproot poverty and create a more just and fraternal world" (No. 1161).

The Puebla conference was keenly aware of the conflicts, tensions, and dangers of this route for the church-institution as such, as conceived in its present form. It even discerns the threat of deviation from its proper function by dilution in pure political activism.

The final document is full of warnings and alarms: certain political alternatives, certain ways to struggle, are reprehensible. Only the future will tell what concrete repercussions, what specific routes of change, and what alternative political models the faithful of Latin America will settle upon most meaningfully.

An Unupdated Left

This indisputable effervescence, along with the less noticeable importance of the religious world for the class struggle of Latin America in the years ahead, has been comprehended in good time by the right, but not yet so well by the left. The right, pragmatic through and through, is accustomed to being ruled by the facts; the left, grown fond of theories that have hardened into dogmas, prefers to try to reduce troublesome facts to mere deceptive appearances.

And so it comes about that the left is a bit behind in making important adjustments in its grasp of the political meaning of the religious phenomenon. But even here a beginning is being made. Not a few individuals, faced with the clear fact of Christian participation in popular struggles, now admit the possibility that religion on our continent may significantly contribute to the defeat of the prevailing system and its current disorder. Others, in spite of their dogmas to the contrary (based on their interpretation of the outstanding facts of at least sixteen centuries of Christian history), are at any rate beginning to concede the benefit of the doubt. Finally, there are even those who say that it is only with the massive support of Christians, motivated by their resources in the gospel to come to grips with the inhuman reality confronting them, that today's oppressed minorities—religious persons by and large—will be able to build a new society of liberation and human dignity.

This whole picture, shifting and somewhat unpredictable as it has been over the past thirty years, calls for attentive observation of the facts, as well as for the development of theoretical categories that will be adequate to the interpretation of these facts, with a view to positive contributions to a task to be carried out with, and from within, the oppressed classes.

The left, especially the Marxist left, used to have a tradition with respect to the problem of religion that harks back to Marx's own description of it in his *Critique of the Philosophy of the Right:*

Religion is the sigh of the oppressed creature, the heart of a heartless world, the spirit of a situation deprived of spirit. It is the people's opium. . . .
The abolition of religion as the people's illusory beatitude is necessary for their real beatitude.

Today there are even those in the Marxist world who ask whether this is a *sociological* affirmation, based on positive observation, and hence hypothetical and open to contradiction by the further course of history, or a *metaphysical* statement on the essence of the social meaning of religion, based on certain important but partial findings of nineteenth-century thought and nevertheless claimed to be absolute and eternal. I think that in good, solid logic, if one wishes to maintain the character of this affirmation as a scientific statement, the reduction of religion to an opium of the people will have to be subjected to the tests of past and present history, and hence be open to correction. We shall have to take our station along the road of history, and see by the facts whether the "heart of a heartless world" can become the motive power for building a world with a heart.

Religion and a New World

What is at issue is whether, from a point of departure in specific forms of understanding and living religion with and from within the oppressed classes, a struggle can and should be undertaken for "the abolition of religion as the people's illusory beatitude." We have yet to see whether indeed believers cannot fully identify with the people's battle for their genuine well-being without thereby losing the sense of the transcendent and the metahistorical that is characteristic of all religion. To put it in another way, is it really impossible for religion to be the nucleus of popular resistance, something hope can feed on, a transforming goad to build a new world, in concert with all who long for, and on behalf of all who need, a new world?

This is the theme of the present book. The author approaches it with the depth and clarity of the sociologist, analyzing the social and political implications of the religious phenomenon from the viewpoint of class struggles. Ineluctably, new facts set new hypotheses afoot here, and new theories of interpretation. Of necessity, this work has been the contribution of someone deeply committed to the cause of the oppressed in Latin America. Appropriately, it has been undertaken with sufficient "scientific cool" to see things as they are, and not simply as one might wish them to be. By the same token, it has been undertaken with a sufficiently long and broad experience of the religious world from within, and passion for the struggle of the people, to be the work of one who grasps from personal experience that religion can be a force for that people's resistance and combat.

In his long quest for light, the author has placed his Christian experience in the scales of rational judgment, and come to the enthusiastic discovery of the Marxist theory of religion. But he did not stop there. He kept on investigating Marxism, and carried his studies into the field of the sociology of religion:

> The sociology of religions has helped me grasp a series of mistakes, errors, and exaggerations present in the Marxist theory of religion, and at the same time has supplied me with the tools necessary to move from theory to a concrete analysis of religious phenomena in a determinate society.

The mature fruit of these findings (upon which the author has already given us two other voluminous studies, as well as numerous articles in specialized periodicals) is the present book—"a radical reformulation of the Marxist theory of religion, with a view to beginning to sketch the outlines of a response to some questions arising out of a malaise" besetting the author. The malaise is a profound one, and common to millions of Latin American Christians. They will agree with the author when he says:

> Since 1965, I have been troubled by the existence of certain Latin American societies in which the majority of human beings are subjected to a harsh regimen organized to fatten the bank accounts of local and foreign minorities. This troubles me to the point of incapacitating me for any understanding or living of my gospel faith except within the struggle against this social regimen, which I perceive as unjust *and*

transformable. And it troubles me to the point where I cannot submissively cross my arms in the face of certain allegedly "Christian" attitudes and traditions that appear to me to be an antievangelical instrumentalization of the church in the service of social injustice.

I must say that, in spite of a certain familiarity I had with this subject, and my anxiety and human dedication with respect to the task of building a liberative Christianity, I have found in this book a very cohesive, solid, new wealth of material. And the author has done his work without narcissism or grandstanding. Those who, be they believers or no, care anything about the liberation of the oppressed classes—a pending liberation, and one fraught with obstacles—in these so indisputably religious lands, will find many an element of novel analysis here. And those Christians, clergy, and bishops included, who seek to become conscious of the social role they so often play (against their explicit intentions and desires) in the service of a social order that cannot be blessed by followers of Christ, will find the same.

The great richness of the theoretical contribution of these pages stems from the fact that the author makes his sociological approach to religions in its duplexity as *product* of social relationships and as autonomous, nuclear *producer* of social relationships. Accordingly, religion is analyzed in its twofold potentiality: as the "potential *conservative* function of church-type religious systems" and as the "potential *revolutionary* function of church-type religious systems."

The religious sphere can be considered as *product* of social conflicts, but at the same time it is a relatively autonomous *terrain* of social conflicts. That is, social conflicts have a profound influence on religion, but religion in its turn, with its relative autonomy, has its effect upon the conflicts, whether for the reinforcement of the power of the dominating class, or as a delegitimizing force fostering the construction of a new society.

It is with great precision that Otto Maduro analyzes "how the dominant classes have both the interest and the material means to place religion at the service of the extension, intensification, and consolidation of the dominance exercised by these same classes." And at the same time, he studies the opposite phenomenon, constructing the following hypothesis:

Under determinate social conditions, and in the presence of a determinate internal situation in the religious area, certain religious practices, teachings and institutions perform, in class societies, a role that is favorable to the autonomous development of certain subordinate classes, and to the reinforcement of their alliances against domination.

To those of us Christians who, by reason of our evangelical convictions, believe that we may in no wise contribute to the domination of humans by humans—because we would thereby be denying our faith in the gospel of Jesus—it is of immeasurable interest to understand the multiplicity of ways, sometimes subtle and sometimes not so subtle, in which we become very useful instruments in the hands of dominant minorities. Those of us who feel called by Puebla to resist our own potential role as oppressors will do very well to read this book.

Those who do not identify with the religious world, but who do seek change and liberation for the dominated classes of society—a society which, in spite of all, continues to be a religious one—have equal need of this book. They have a need to understand the contributions that believers may be able to make—either to the revolution, or to the maintenance of the established order. And finally, by reading this book, the Latin American left can have its eyes opened to the forms of behavior and activity by which it all too frequently raises obstacles to a positive contribution on the part of believers, and to the incorporation of our national religious majorities in the cause of the liberation of the people.

Luis Ugalde, S.J.
Provincial of the Jesuit Order in Venezuela

PREFACE

"Understanding is to be able to remake; it is power."
Jean Ullmo

I am a Latin American Catholic. This, together with certain particularities of my personal history, makes me especially sensitive to many aspects of Latin American Catholicism. I was born in 1945. Thus, whether I like it or not, I belong to a generation that has been profoundly affected by the Second Vatican Council, by the CELAM meetings in Medellín in 1968 and in Puebla in 1979, by the Cuban and the Nicaraguan revolutions, and by the mighty achievements of Father Camilo Torres and Mons. Oscar Romero, among hundreds of contemporary Catholic martyrs in Latin America.

I am incapable of remaining impassive vis-à-vis the millions of human beings in Latin America today who suffer under the yoke of a social organization whose only purpose is to fatten the bank accounts of a minority. Nor am I capable of hearing the gospel as a call to impassivity. My own personal conviction is that to be a Catholic in Latin America today implies a radical, constant, and collective commitment to the struggle for a community of free brothers and sisters on our continent.

But—likewise and in equal measure—I am aware of the fact that our church in Latin America has established such bonds with the powerful that its preaching and activity often serve to prevent persons from making the commitment the gospel seems to demand. Accordingly, it seems to me, fidelity to the gospel also requires a strenuous, permanent, and communitarian commitment to the struggle to burst the bonds that still lash the church to the chariot of the mighty.

But I know very well that it is not enough to wish for something in order to make it reality. It is not enough to denounce a situation in order to make it vanish. It is not enough to be solidly committed to a struggle in order for it to have a successful outcome. No, all this is insufficient. We have to come to *know*—to know how and why things have come to this pass in the church and in society. We have to learn what changes are possible—in the short, the intermediate, and the long term—and learn how such changes are feasible in the church and in society. And it is probable that one could learn something in this regard from those who have devoted their whole lives to delving into and trying to comprehend the relationships between church and society.

These were the anxieties and suspicions that filled my head and my heart as I set out for Louvain in May 1971. I went there with the somewhat vague idea that Marxism, in spite of its blind metaphysical atheism, contained some elements that could be useful for an understanding of why and how things had come to their present state in the church and in society, and for determining how and what changes are possible today in the church and society in Latin America. And I think that I was not altogether mistaken, and that my stay in Louvain was well worthwhile for the objectives I had set myself.

No, I had not been altogether mistaken. But things were not as easy as they had seemed to me before I began my studies there.

After a few somewhat awkward attempts to determine a theme for my Master's dissertation in philosophy, I settled on the Marxist theory of religion. Why? Surely because there were concerns and leanings in my own subjectivity that found a point of convergence there. After all, did not the church often condemn movements for social transformation because they were thought to disguise Marxist atheism? Was it not on Marxist atheism that the church concentrated a great part of its critique of socialism? And on the other hand, was not Marxism the inspiration of the bravest battlers for the social transformation of Latin America? Was not Marxism the political theory that most bitterly denounced the utilization of the church in the service of the private interests of the powerful?

And so in August 1972, I set to work. The first step was to try to sort out what the Marxist critique of religion consisted in, so as to be able to see, in a second step, whether or not Marxist theory furnished any elements that would be useful for an understanding of why and how relationships between church and society had reached the state in which we find them in Latin America today, and for learning what changes are possible in these relationships today and how to attain them. The result of these efforts was my book *Marxismo y Religión*. Here, somewhat naively at times (a naivety I sought to correct in the Introduction and the Conclusions), I attempted to make explicit and systematize the theory of religion as found in the most relevant writings of Marx and Engels.

This first effort, concluded in May 1973, was not completely disappointing. I managed to reach my immediate objective, in part at least: to come to an understanding of what the Marxist theory of religion consisted in. And I even began to grasp that indeed Marxism could help me understand the relationships between church and society, at least in some respects: how class conflicts influence a religion and its train of thought, and, particularly, how and why the domination of some classes by others has an influence on the religious worldview developing in a class society. Not a huge discovery, perhaps, but it was something, and for the moment it was enough for me. Besides, my research had provided me with a familiarity with the pertinent literature. Hence, after two years, I was able to publish my article "Marxist

Analysis and Sociology of Religions. An Outline of International Bibliography up to 1975," in *Social Compass*.

Still, my early work had developed in such a way that I now faced two problems, to which I could see no immediate response. First, how could I move from Marxist theory of religion to a concrete analysis of the religious phenomena in a determinate society? Secondly, why this mutual rejection by Marxists and believers? The first problem led me to a study of the sociology of religions. The second became the theme of my doctoral dissertation in philosophy.

And so from 1973 to 1976 I continued to plumb the subject of Marxist theory of religion. The sociology of religions helped me recognize a series of shortcomings, errors, and exaggerations in that theory. At the same time, it provided me with what I needed to move from what was solid in this theory to a concrete analysis of the religious phenomena of a determinate society. For nearly four years, then, I concentrated the sociological aspect of my study on the principal defects in Marxist theory of religion. I sought to overcome them with the aid of the reflections of Antonio Gramsci and Hugues Portelli, Max Weber and Pierre Bourdieu, and Maurice Godelier, François Houtart, and Jean Remy.

This was probably the most fertile period in my research—not only because of the research papers I wrote then (which are now being revised for publication), but also and especially because of the theories and analyses with which I came into contact. I think they made a considerable contribution to answering the questions that had brought me to Louvain: How and why have relationships between church and society in Latin America come to their present state? What changes are possible in these relationships? How are these changes feasible—how can they be brought about?

During this same period, as I sought to clarify the problem of mutual rejection by Marxists and Christians, I was compelled to study the historical origin of Marxist theory—the economic, political, intellectual, and religious conditions that made it possible for this theory to develop in the first half of the nineteenth century. I also had to look for a sociological explanation for Marxist atheism and church-related anticommunism. The result was my 300-page doctoral dissertation "La cuestión religiosa en el Engels premarxista." Here I attempted to demonstrate what my research had suggested: that the mutual rejection of Marxists and Christians formed part of the very problem that had brought me to Louvain—that of the relationships between church and society, and their mutual conditioning. In other words, I attempted to show that the alleged or assumed incompatibility between these two institutionalized worldviews, Marxist and Christian, is not so much "essential" as it is *historical*. And perhaps it is historically surmountable as well.

After all, my attempt to use Marxism for solving my politico-religious questions—questions arising out of my gospel commitment to the liberation of the oppressed in Latin America—had now led me to act, think, and feel somewhat as a "Marxist Christian." Hence I was no longer capable of understanding this combination as a contradiction or absurdity. On the contrary, now it seemed practically a necessity. So I had to force myself to see how far it was possible to continue to be what I now felt I had been becoming, with peaks and plateaus, since about 1970—a Marxist Christian—and if it was possible, just how to go about it.

Thus it was that, after the completion of my sociological studies in 1975 and my philosophical studies in 1977, there remained at least one more task: the systemization, in a kind of "theoretical framework," of the paths I had discovered in the course of my Louvain research. This had to be done in order to answer the questions that had brought me to Louvain in the first place: How and why have Latin American church and society come to the point where they are today? What changes are possible, today, in each? And how can these changes be realized? If my study of the sociology of religions in general, and of the Marxist theory of religion in particular, had been of any use, I thought I ought to be able to write an orderly exposition of certain ideas that could make some response to these questions.

The pages that follow carry into effect precisely this attempt to systematize certain ideas, which, it seems to me, could be of very great help in the task of solving the old, insistent problems of those who ask the same questions as I. It is not a study of the thought of a particular author, although it is, indirectly, an attempt to reformulate the Marxist theory of religion—by correcting and broadening it.

The reformulation it seeks to be is the reformulation of *one theme* in the Marxist theory of religion: the interrelationships between the religious field and class conflicts. And the reformulation has a historical point of departure: the liberation struggles of the Latin American peoples in the final quarter of the twentieth century. Further, it is a reformulation constructed on a particular theologico-political position: the theology of liberation as understood and lived by a "Christian for socialism." Finally, it is a reformulation carried out by a human being who has a precise biographical definition: myself, with my personal inclinations and aversions.

An inflexibly orthodox Marxist will find little of his or her venerated Marx here. And little do I care, for I have not meant to be "faithful to Marx" for a single moment. I have simply tried, as a Latin American Catholic today, to find answers for a few questions I have in the sociology of religion. Marx's answers, sketched in 1848, are no longer acceptable unless we reformulate them. Our context is too different from his. And an adequate reformulation of his questions and answers will mean correcting whatever calls for correction (and this is a great deal), eliminating whatever calls for elimination (and this is also a great deal), and recasting much of the rest from top to bottom.

PART I

The Problem of a Latin American
Sociology of Religions

Chapter One

WHAT DO WE MEAN
BY "RELIGIONS"?

The word "religions" appears in the title of Part I. It would seem that we have a clear notion of what this word means. But are we really sure? Or does our frequent use of the word only reflect a *presumption* that we have a clear idea of its meaning? It is possible that this is true. Let us examine this possibility for a moment.

If we ask someone what the word "religion" means, he or she may well reply, "belief in God." At least this is how the word has ordinarily been used in Spanish for centuries, apparently, and this is how it is used today. In fact, we can look the word up in any dictionary of modern Spanish, and there, sure enough, we will find that *religión* means "belief in God." But in fact are things really that simple?

Let us keep in mind that Spanish is but one of hundreds of living languages in the twentieth century. Let us also recall that Spanish is a language with a history—that it has not existed from all eternity. Further, let us keep in account that the history of this language is intimately bound up with *one* particular religion—Catholicism. Will not this intimate link between the Spanish language and the Catholic Church have left a deep mark on the meaning of the word *religión* in Spanish?

True, the word "religion" does not exist only in Spanish. It is originally a Latin word, *religio*, and its history antedates Christianity. Its etymology is obscure. Some think it is related to *re-ligare:* to "re-fasten," to "tie tightly again"—in which case its etymological meaning will be something like "the strict and faithful observance of a commitment by which one has bound oneself." Others, however, think it comes from *re-legere:* to "re-read," or to "interpret literally" (a manuscript, for instance). Finally, still others believe *religio* derives from *re-eligere*, meaning to "re-elect," to "re-choose," to "accept definitively" (a way of life, for example). Even its etymological meaning is unclear, equivocal.

What is sure is that the same word exists in many of today's languages, and that Spanish usually translates it as *religión*. It is *religião* in Portuguese, *réli-jion* in Antillean Creole, *religion* in English and French, *Religion* in German,

3

religione in Italian, *religió* in Catalan, and so on, in a score of other languages. But these languages constitute only a minority of all those used by the human species, and their speakers make up less than half the population of our planet.

The word "religion," in its various spellings and pronunciations, and meaning more or less the same thing from language to language, occurs especially in languages whose history is closely linked with the history of Christianity. Hundreds of other languages do not have a word of their own that would satisfactorily translate our word "religion" in its common usage. And so it turns out that the word "religion," like all words, is historically, geographically, culturally, and demographically *situated* within a language. It is this *particular stationing* that gives it its meaning—a rich meaning, no doubt, but one that, by reason of its vital particularity, is complex, variable, ambiguous, and obscure.

The majority of Spanish-speaking persons might well respond that this is far from true; indeed it is simply false that the meaning of the word *religión* is "complex, variable, ambiguous, and obscure." On the contrary, its meaning is fixed, simple, univocal, and transparent, we will be told. *Religión* means "belief in God." Well, then, let us take seven persons whose language is Spanish: (1) an illiterate *campesino*—landworker, "peasant"—in the Venezuelan Amazon, (2) a native of the Esequibo region in Guyana, (3) a Madrid attorney, (4) a Philippine businessman, (5) a Chicano farmhand in California, (6) a Puerto Rican biologist, (7) a policewoman in Santiago, Cuba. Now, let us suppose that these persons have rather different religious beliefs. The Amazonian, let us say, is a Catholic, the Guyanese a polytheist, the Spaniard a Mason, the Filipino a Buddhist, the Chicano a Moony, the Puerto Rican a spiritist of the Kardecist cult, and the Cuban an atheist.

Among these seven Spanish-speaking persons, will we find total agreement that "religion" means "belief in God"? It is not very likely. And we are not referring to whether they think belief in God is true or false, good or bad (although this can also have an influence on their concept of religion), but, very simply, what meaning each assigns to the *word*.

And the plot thickens. Even in one and the same language, religious denomination, time, city, social class, age, and occupation—for example, in a group of Jesuit theologians in Caracas—we would find that the term "religion" has different meanings, even mutually exclusive meanings. And then, even supposing that all the Jesuit theologians of Caracas would agree to define religion as "belief in God" (which is not very likely), it is almost impossible that all of them would agree on the meaning of "belief" and of "God."

Finally, the problem would become still more complicated were we to ask the following questions, one by one: Is Rosicrucianism a religion? What about Masonry? Voodoo? The María Lionza cult? And what about atheism? —for there are those who hold that, at bottom, atheism is a religion, whereas others, quite the contrary, think that atheism is exactly the opposite of religion.

The fact is that, generally speaking, "religion" means what we were taught it meant when we were small—together with certain other elements we have later come to understand as pertaining to the meaning of religion. But these other elements *vary*. They vary from age to age, from society to society, from place to place, from social class to social class, and . . . well, of course . . . from religion to religion!

Dictionaries reflect usage, the "common meaning" of a word, for one given time, one society, and one socio-geographical and ideological milieu— generally an influential, minority.[7] This is what dictionaries do with the word "religion." But the historico-social variations of meaning—the de facto meanings, all told—are so great, the contradictory usages of a term in society so obvious, and the wealth and complexity of a word's meaning so enormous in a case like this, that the apparent simplicity and clarity of a dictionary definition, instead of helping us, only obscures what "religion" can mean for our specific purposes here and now.

Other Approaches to a Definition

Perhaps the thing for us to do at this point would be either to make an exhaustive examination of the uses of the term "religion" until we can find a common pattern, or else, without further preliminaries, elaborate a working ("operational" and "scientific") definition of the term that will be adequate for our purposes. Evidently, the first alternative is impossible; we shall not attempt it.[8]

The other alternative—the elaboration of a working definition adequate for purposes of this study—is doubtless possible, but certain rough spots would remain, and there would be no way of smoothing them all out. Any working definition of religion, however vague, would sooner or later encounter the objection that it *includes* elements that many persons would never accept as being part of religion. And, by the same token, it would encounter the opposite objection that it *excludes* elements that just as many other persons consider essential to religion.

Besides, we cannot propose a totally arbitrary definition of religion—as a physicist can when defining "mass," for example—because we want to make at least some reference to the phenomena that persons experience and perceive as "religious." And we should have to do this even at the price of excluding some traits and including others that would violate the "common meaning" of the word.

So what shall we do? Skip the definition of "religion" and plunge right in without one? Perhaps when we have finished our investigation of the sociological problem of religions, a satisfactory definition will emerge by itself, even though we shall have taken as our point of departure a vague and obscure acceptation of the term. Perhaps. But experience tends to discredit the likelihood.[9]

And then too, the reader of a study such as this one has a perfect right, and even the need, to have some sort of definition as the work begins, even if it is purely provisional, even if it is intended simply as an orientation to what the author of the study means by "religion." What can we do to satisfy this right and meet this need?

The word "religion," let us repeat, like any word in any language, is a word that is *situated*—historically, geographically, culturally, and demographically—within a given linguistic community. And it is this *particular situation* that lends the word its meaning—a rich meaning in this case, but therefore a complex, variable, ambiguous, and confused meaning, too.

Our "Relatively Arbitrary" Definition

And so, here in the midst of this "jungle of signification," let us begin to work out a relatively arbitrary definition of the term "religion." I say "relatively" arbitrary, because my experience of religion, together with my researches in the sociology of religion,[10] will somewhat reduce the arbitrary quality of the definition. And I hope the reduction will be sufficient to render the result of our selection adequate for the purposes of this study, and perform some of the functions a definition is usually expected to perform.[11]

With all this having been said, we shall now state what the word "religion" will mean throughout the coming pages. It will mean *a structure of discourses* and practices common to a social group, referring to certain forces (personified or not, multiple or unified) that believers consider as anterior and superior to their natural and social surroundings,[12] in whose regard they express their sense of a certain dependency (through creation, control, protection, threat, or the like), and before which they consider themselves obligated to a particular pattern of conduct in society.[13]*

Why did we not spare ourselves the long discussion, then, and simply put this definition at the beginning of the chapter and get on with our investigation? For one sole reason: because definitions (especially in the social sciences) that spare the reader any explicitation of the *problematical* character of their terms serve only to evade and conceal the history and conflicts of every scholarly discipline, as if they had no importance. For us, on the contrary, because we intend to pursue the specific problem of religion as *a complex field of mediation of social conflicts* in Latin America, it was important to underscore the socially conflictive, historical character of the definition of the term "religion."

But—and here is one last objection that might be raised—this definition of "religion" is neither a dictionary definition, nor a theological definition, nor a philosophical definition, but merely a *sociological* definition of the term. And a sociological definition lops off, right from the start, a good part of the religious phenomenon, which for many is precisely the *essential* part of religion—faith, grace, revelation, conversion, mystical experience, the word

---

* Henceforth I shall use the word "discourse" as meaning the oral *and* written material produced by an individual, a group, or an institution.

of God, and so on. This is true. Our definition is not intended to be an "essential definition," a definition of the essence, of religion. Nor therefore does it seek to be the only, or the best, or the most complete, definition of what religion is "in itself." Certainly not.

This definition of religion is, then, a strictly *sociological* one, or at least this is all it is intended to be. As such, it claims to embrace but *one aspect* of the inexhaustible wealth of religious phenomena—the sociologically relevant aspect of these phenomena.

As a *partial* definition, then—besides being provisional and relatively arbitrary—it is intended to serve as an instrument of orientation in a sociological study of religion in Latin America. The fact that we place it at the beginning of our study does not mean we are going to maintain it dogmatically throughout the whole investigation. Its function is precisely to situate us, as we start out, in a particular perspective—a sociological one—with respect to phenomena that can be considered "religious" phenomena.

The reason why I presented my definition only at the end of a long excursus on the historical and social character of the meaning of *any* word, is that my purpose, from the very beginning, is to narrow the meaning of religion—along with even the *word* "religion"—to its function as a *social* field and a *social* medium of communication and struggle. Thus our sociological definition is "partialized."

This leads us to another question. Perplexed at the narrowness and particularity of our approach to such a broad and rich thing as religion, there is something else we have to treat: What is this thing called sociology? What is *its* definition?

Chapter Two

WHAT IS "SOCIOLOGY"?

We have used the term "sociology" in the title of this part of our book. We have defined religion from a "sociological" viewpoint. This book is a study in the "sociology" of religions. But what is sociology?

The answer would seem to be obvious. It is a science. It is a science whose object of study is society. Thus sociology would be "the science of society." And yet—once again—things are not as simple as they seem at first sight.

"Sociology" is a relatively new word—a good deal newer than is the word "religion" in any of the various languages in which they both occur. "Sociology" was born in 1839, in the French language, under the pen of the scholar Auguste Comte. Thus it is less than a century and a half old—even younger in Spanish. Its etymology, unlike that of "religion," is quite simple: it comes from *societas* (Latin for "society") and *logos*, the Greek root that has come to mean "science." There it is again: the "science of society." How could anything be simpler or clearer?

But what does "science" mean? What does "society" mean? All the professionals who "do sociology," or "teach sociology" may well agree on this elementary definition of sociology—as the "science of society"—but it would be difficult to get them to agree on what "science" is, or what they understand by "society." And indeed there are in reality many forms—different forms, even opposing forms—of understanding and "doing" sociology, of understanding and doing science, and of understanding and studying what society is.

There are many schools, many currents of thought, in sociology today. Each understands and practices sociology in its own way. We could undertake a more or less exhaustive inventory of the principal schools of sociology today, and list the characteristic traits of what each of them understands and practices under the name of "sociology." Then we could work out a sort of "compromise definition" of what sociology is. We could, but we shall not. In the first place, this has already been done, more or less adequately.[14] Secondly, it would go far beyond the limits of this book. And finally, I do not think it would contribute much to our purpose here—which is to give as clear as possible an explanation of what we are going to be meaning when we use the term "sociology."

8

One of the things that makes "sociology" look like a clear, unambiguous, and stable term, to the professional as well as to the neophyte, is the fact that there are schools and institutes, centers and associations, degrees and diplomas, textbooks, surveys, and research projects, in "sociology." At least, this is their formal, public label. But we must not allow this "evidence" to pull the wool over our eyes. Great is the confusion, and abundant the contradictions, about what professionals in sociology ought to understand and practice under this label.

The methods, the object, the purposes, the scope, the limits—*everything*, in fact—about sociology is the subject of confusion and disputes. Why? Is it not because the same *social* circumstances that originally occasioned the birth of sociology continue today, making of sociology a sphere of confusion and debate? I suspect that this is indeed the case. Let us, then, review the social conditions in which sociology originated, in order to see how far they can explain the *problems* of sociology today, in two senses: (1) the *themes* that sociology studies, and (2) the *difficulties* that it encounters in studying these themes.

A European Matrix

Sociology was born in Europe, in the nineteenth century—a century of change, inventions, migrations, wars, revolutions, and social conflicts and discoveries. It was a century in which western Europe, where sociology began, saw change after change coming at it with a velocity and a violence never before known. Social changes, political changes, technological, philosophical, industrial, economic, military, religious, theological, hygienic, and geographical changes followed on one another's heels with a continuous, dizzying entanglement, in England, France, and Germany.

The European nobility, which had had the control and reaped the profits of the Old World for centuries, now saw its sway threatened and mutilated—a sway that monarchs and feudal lords had thought everlasting. The bourgeoisie—that enterprising, innovative, daring "middle class" of the bourgs, the cities—which until then had been looked down upon and made use of by the nobility, saw its opportunities for wealth and power waxing. It grasped at the power of the nobility, and took it for itself in all areas.

The collapse of the nobility and the rise of the bourgeoisie, further accelerated by the boom of the Industrial Revolution, drove the workers and artisans of the countryside to the cities, where they ended up in the sweatshops, on the streets, in the prisons, shelters, and hospitals. Thus was born, violently, a working class. And no sooner was it born than it was battling in the city streets, striking, sabotaging, demanding bread, work, housing, suffrage, laws to protect its rights, and other forms of redress.

It was a century in which the Christian churches—French Catholicism, German Protestantism, and the Church of England—saw their power curtailed, their wealth expropriated, their schools snatched away from them, their presence diminished in the newborn mass medium of the press, the number of their faithful reduced, their armies disbanded, and their efforts to mold the mentality of citizens impeded in every way. In succession, anticlerical, agnostic, and atheistic philosophies multiplied, sects proliferated, and opposed and disputatious currents of thought held forth from ecclesiastical chairs of learning. Theology's place was taken by the natural sciences—the positive sciences, the exact sciences. The press took more and more account of the latter and less and less of the former.

A great part of the funds that disappeared from the sacristy turned up in the hands of inventors, scientific researchers, and science teachers. Astronomy, chemistry, mathematics, medicine, physics, and botany, with their material benefits of more or less direct application in the field of industrial production, began to replace—in prestige and in capital resources—dogmatic theology, moral theology, church history, biblical exegesis, and liturgical studies. Quantification, prediction, experimentation, and technological inventions became the new altars of a new dominant class. And a new era was born—the era of capitalist industrialization, and the era of working-class struggles against this new form of exploitation of human labor.

The Founders of Sociology

In that century of such rapid and bloody transformations and confrontations, certain persons devoted themselves to reflection upon society—upon its changes and its conflicts. And they were persons of their age through and through. They lived in the midst of its changes themselves, and were personally concerned with its inherent conflicts. They were individuals made to the image and likeness of the new dominant class, the bourgeoisie—enterprising, disciplined, fairly well-off, university-educated, estranged from the church, and completely won over by the achievements of the new sciences. Comte, Saint-Simon, Proudhon, Quetelet, Tocqueville, Marx, Engels, Durkheim, Weber, Sombart, Tawney, Troeltsch, and others, were of their number. Living in France, Germany, and England, they had seen with their own eyes the historico-social cataclysm that was shaking the Europe of the nineteenth century. And having seen it, they began to attempt to understand and explain the changes and shocks with which their own society daily trembled.

They tried to discover the causes and mechanisms of those changes and shocks, in order to predict their results, in order to be able to design procedures that could influence, in one way or another, the alterations and conflicts of European society in their time. They sought to understand their society in terms of the type of knowledge that had begun to impose itself in its appropriate field—that of the natural, positive, exact *sciences*, with their direct observation of material reality, quantification, experimentation, induction, hypothetical explanation, prediction. And so, by their efforts to understand their own society, and to influence the course of future events, these individuals, all in their own fashion, created a new discipline—sociology, the "science" of society, its changes, its conflicts.

Society and the Sociologist

Sociology, then, was originally an effort of description and analysis, with a view to *understanding*—in the scientific categories then in vogue—European society in the process of industrialization, *explaining* the origins, changes, and conflicts proper to this process, and *solving*, so far as possible, whatever appeared to each "sociologist" to be the most serious problem of capitalistic industrialization. Their proposals—modest or daring—for the solution of problems were often accompanied by an effort to *predict* the future course of those problems.

In comparison with history—a knowledge of society's past—sociology might be thought of as a knowledge of society's present.

But the very conflicts that sociology seeks to describe and analyze, understand and explain, predict and resolve, were soon seen to be present within sociology itself. After all, a sociologist wants to find an explanation for a conflict, its genesis and its outcome, rendering a judgment on society and its evolution, and making suggestions for action to be taken to solve problems. But in undertaking all these things, the sociologist will in one way or another be obliged to take part in them. Consciously or unconsciously, explicitly or implicitly, and like it or not, every sociologist takes a position in favor of capitalism or against it, side by side with the bourgeoisie or in confrontation with it, for or against the working class. And so, point by point, this young discipline called sociology found itself sketching its points of internal conflict as its various currents of thought coursed into one another.

Is misery and conflict inherent in, or incidental to, capitalistic society as such? Is the division of society into opposing classes eternal or historical? Is it of primary or secondary importance? Indeed, is it fact or fiction? Is capitalism a natural form of harmonious cooperation, or is it an exploitation imposed by the interaction of unequal forces? Is private property something essential to human nature as such, or is it a mere contingency of history? These are some of the various points of conflict that have confronted sociologists since the very birth of this scientific discipline.

Such points of conflict reveal a trait of human society that constitutes, by that very reason, a *difficulty*, a *presupposition*, and a *theme* of sociology. In point of fact, *society is opaque, not transparent,* to the observer.[15] The genesis, organization, functioning, and transformations of society cannot be grasped or comprehended easily or directly. All the more reason, then, to undertake a methodical, thorough, comparative, documented, concrete study of society—that is, all the more reason for having a *"science* of society." But this is also reason in itself why explanations will vary from observer to observer, to the point where agreement among all observers will not only be difficult, but impossible.

This is also why, more than in practically any other discipline, even including history, sociologists, inasmuch as they are studying their own environment, are judge of, and part of, the sociological process itself. Sociologists not only observe social struggles; they are—willy-nilly—involved in them. Even against their will, sociologists observe these struggles from the positions they occupy in them.

Thus more than in nearly any other discipline, in sociology the observer is part of the object observed. More than in practically any other discipline, the observer's mental schemata influence what he or she is capable of observing, and the manner in which it is observed. More than in almost any other discipline, the observer finds it difficult to be cold and objective. And this is why, among other reasons, sociologists find it difficult to explain, and predict with any high degree of probability, the behavior of their object of study—human society.

In coming to realize the existence of these intrinsic obstacles to sociological knowledge, the founders of sociology, more or less explicitly in each case, encountered another trait of human society—which thereupon came to constitute a *difficulty*, a *presupposition*, and a *theme* of sociology. They discovered that the spontaneous consciousness we have of our life in society—our spontaneous consciousness of its causes, for example, or of its mechanisms, or of its consequences—does not afford a scientifically acceptable explanation of life in society. It is almost the other way around: it is this spontaneous consciousness that needs to be explained sociologically. The genesis, development, and social functioning of these superficial explanations demand a sociological explanation themselves.

In other words, we find ourselves confronted with the fact that *the underlying motives of our conduct in society—like its results and consequences—are not spontaneously or directly knowable.* On the contrary, the explanations we generally give ourselves to explain our comportment in society appear to be one of the *products* of our social life, and, far from revealing the nature of our society's functioning, they constitute an *obstacle* to the scientific understanding of society.[16]

So here is yet another reason for engaging in a critical, cautious, and perspicacious study of our society. In other words, here is another reason for "doing" sociology. But at the same time it is a reason for us sociologists to oblige ourselves to be suspicious of our own explanations—however spontaneous, attractive, "evident," and acceptable to our audience they might be.

The Specificity of Society and of Sociology

As we are beginning to appreciate, sociology is—to an enormous extent—the product of a *specific* society. It is so in several senses:

- Sociology is a *consequence* of the convergence of the problems and the mental schemata that have arisen with capitalistic industrialization.
- Sociology is an *attempt to explain* these problems and mental schemata.
- Sociology is an *effort to resolve* some of the serious difficulties generated in the convergence of these problems and mental schemata.
- Sociology is therefore also one more *terrain* for the irruption of the problems and mental schemata that have developed at the heart of capitalistic industrialization.

Thus, sociology finds itself in a difficult situation. But it is a situation that cannot be avoided. How can one escape it without simply fleeing present society—and thereby renouncing any active participation in its dynamics, whether to revolutionize it or, on the contrary, to take advantage of it?

Sociology is indeed—or at least seeks to be—the "science of society." And sociology is above all the science of *present* society—a systematic, patient, laborious effort to get to the bottom of the origins, the functioning, the conflicts, and the alternatives of present society. It will be an effort whose findings will be documented, and seriously and scientifically founded, and hence communicable to other researchers, who can test them, and thus apply them to other situations and other perspectives. It will be an effort to formulate conditional predictions that have real meaning, and to propose feasible alternatives. It will be an effort to orientate human groups in the midst of their social conflicts, to reduce the frustrations and the ill-advised actions that are the fruit of society's uncertainty, society's ignorance of the things that socially condition it.

The specificity of sociology as the "science of society" is traditionally maintained to be *the explanation of the social by the social.*[17] That is, for sociology, "every social phenomenon is in some fashion the product of other social phenomena."[18] Sociology, then, is based on the principle that every properly human phenomenon that arises within a society (every "social phenomenon") is the result of other phenomena that likewise arise within that society. These social phenomena (or social facts, or social processes) must therefore find an explanation *within society itself*—that is, without recourse to any extrasocial or metasocial explanation.

Consequently, sociology is a science of society that attempts to explain social phenomena exclusively on the basis of other social phenomena. A sociological explanation of social facts will *not*, therefore, invoke causes that are *supernatural* (providence or fate, for instance), *moral* (the goodness or badness of an individual, group, or system), *natural* (instinct, climate, heredity, etc.), merely *personal* (the intelligence or will of a leader, the complexes or other psychological traits of a person), or even *interpersonal* (such as personal interaction, a conspiracy, or the like).

Sociology, then, is a science of society that seeks to understand and describe social processes (including individual conduct within society) in order to analyze and explain them on the basis of the *relationships* that individuals and groups establish among themselves (generally in an unconscious, unintentional, involuntary manner) within their society. This is the object of sociology: *social relationships*.[19] That is, the object of sociology consists of the relationships that individuals and groups set, up among themselves in a more or less stable fashion, independently of their conscious will. Sociology attempts to explain these social relationships from the exclusive point of view of their *social* character.

It is not that sociology has discovered, invented, or dogmatically imposed the principle that the social aspect of social relationships is their only possible explanation. By no means. What happens is that sociology makes an effort not to renounce the insight that gave it birth—the insight that all the relationships that we human beings set up among ourselves are our own work, a human deed, resulting from other relationships with which we ourselves (simultaneously or otherwise) have knotted together various individuals or groups; the insight that the opacity and nonconsciousness of our own social relationships are in large part our work as well, a human deed; the insight that we ourselves, precisely because our social relationships are our own doing, are ultimately capable of undoing, redoing, or transforming our social organization; the insight that the very obstacles we encounter at every step in our attempts to undo, redo, or transform our social relationships are themselves social relationships, which we have manufactured without knowing it, or have forgotten about or blocked out of our consciousness.

In this sense, the profoundly humanistic nature of sociology comes to light.[20] It refuses to explain social processes or individual conduct in society by recourse to causes that escape human knowledge and control. It insists upon finding a *social* explanation for social processes. Nor does it yield to the temptation to explain the social by the individual. Far from it. Sociology takes its point of departure in some manner from the supposition—likewise humanistic—that our life is our *collective* doing, and that therefore our destiny (whether we know it or not, and whether we like it or not) will be our collective doing as well.

This, in broad outline, is our view of sociology. Perhaps now we can return to our definition of "religion" and understand better what we mean when we assert that it is a *sociological* definition of religion.

Chapter Three

WHAT IS SOCIOLOGY OF RELIGIONS?

In chapter 1 we defined religion as "a structure of discourses and practices common to a social group, referring to certain forces (personified or not, multiple or unified) that believers consider as anterior and superior to their natural and social surroundings, in whose regard they express their sense of a certain dependency (through creation, control, protection, threat, or the like), and before which they consider themselves obligated to a particular pattern of conduct in society." We said that this is a "sociological" definition of religion. Why? What is a "sociological" definition of religion?

A sociological definition of religion is a definition of religion as forming part of the general dynamics of society, influencing this dynamics and receiving a determining impact from it. A sociological definition of religion is a definition of religion as a social phenomenon, a social phenomenon immersed in a complex and mobile network of social relationships. That is, a sociological definition of religion is a definition that seeks to gather and express *one aspect* of religion, or of religions—the socio-phenomenal aspect present in every religious fact and deed. Does this mean that, for sociology, religion is *solely and exclusively* a social phenomenon? No, not necessarily. For some sociologists it is, as well as for certain currents of sociological thought. But for my part I think sociology captures one aspect (not *all* aspects) of religious phenomena, one dimension of these phenomena—their sociological dimension.

A sociological discipline is concerned with the study of religious phenomena as social phenomena. It is concerned with the influence exerted by religious institutions on social processes, and with the conditioning imposed by the dynamics of society on the forms and expressions of religion. The discipline concerned with the study of these things is called the "sociology of religion," the "sociology of religions," or—by some sociologists, at least—"religious sociology." When we define religion from a sociological viewpoint —as we have done above—we are already beginning to do sociology of religions.

15

Beginnings

How did the sociology of religions begin? The sociology of religions began with sociology itself. In fact, up to a certain point, with Comte, Marx, and Durkheim, sociology itself began as a sociology of religions. If we glance back at the historical conditions in which sociology was born,[21] we shall understand how the rise of a sociology of religions was possible during the nineteenth century in western Europe.

The innovating processes that agitated and characterized the nineteenth century in Europe were followed by a profound crisis in the churches of the Old World, affecting them in their whole being. Splits, heresies, sects, and theological conflicts rapidly multiplied and diffused—with all the more speed because of the more rapid communications media (railroads, the press, etc.) that were perfected and made more generally available at that same time.

The new power nuclei—bankers, business and industrial potentates—generally despised the larger, established churches, especially in view of their ties to the old dominant nobility and the old landlords of Europe. Thus the young, rising bourgeoisie favored, especially in the press and in the universities, the propagation of anticlerical, antireligious, atheistic, rationalistic, skeptical, agnostic, materialistic, and positivistic ideas. Adrift in the midst of this onslaught, the churches saw their power daily eroding, not only in the spiritual realm, but in the material as well. Church properties were confiscated, schools nationalized, privileges abolished, and ecclesiastical influences on the judicial process reduced to tatters.[22]

What had looked like such a fly-by-night notion—the idea of constructing a science of religions[23]—became for some, in the continually more favorable environment of the nineteenth century, an interesting possibility after all.

Indeed it would not have been so feasible to make religion an *object* of science in the society of near unanimity in matters of religion, and of supreme ecclesiastical authority, that was the society of the Middle Ages. (Later on, of course, clerics came to accept, study, and make use of the sociology of religion.)

But the situation in the society that arose in the nineteenth century in western Europe was very different. It was a society of greatly reduced religious consensus, of public theological quarrels, of remarkable divisions and transformations within the churches, of accelerating erosion of the material and spiritual power of the clergy. It was, in sum, a society that witnessed a drastic diminution in the credibility, importance, and resources of the various churches. In a society such as this, as we have said, it was much more feasible to despoil religion of its untouchable and unquestionable character, and equivalate it to other dimensions of a society that was becoming objectivized and submitted to scientific analysis.

In this atheistic and anticlerical, or at least agnostic, atmosphere of a university-educated, liberal bourgeoisie in France, Germany, and England, where the foundations had been laid for the sociology of religions by the middle of the nineteenth century, now the pioneers appeared—Comte, Marx, Engels, Saint-Simon, Proudhon, and their colleagues.[24] By the end of the same century, in the same circles, the principal pillars of this new science had been erected in the form of the classic works of Weber, Sombart, Durkheim, and Troeltsch.[25]

It is under the auspices of these scholars, then, that a social science of religion was born. That science is an attempt to analyze religions as one dimension, one element, one aspect, of the dynamics of a society. The dimension is a peculiar and particular one, with specific traits and functions, to be sure. But, as in every aspect of society, the founders of sociology saw in religion too a social reality that was suffering under the shocks of economic change, and was having to modify its orientations under the pressure of political events. It was seeing the social and philosophical conflicts of its age taking place on its own terrain. It knew the suffering of internal division brought on by external influences. In a word, the founders of this new discipline saw in religion a reality that, far from wafting above social struggles, political processes, and cultural transformations, was, on the contrary, deeply immersed in and permeated by the new social dynamics.

The Penetration of Institutional Self-Interpretations

A key idea sprang from these scientific analyses of religions in their sociological dimension. In fact, key ideas were many. But perhaps the most interesting and fertile idea of this new discipline known as "the sociology of religions" was this: that the social motives for religious beliefs and practices, the real manner in which such beliefs and practices take shape and develop, and, likewise, the concrete effects of such beliefs and practices on society, generally remain *concealed* as far as the believer is concerned. Instead, believers and their institutions tend to produce spontaneous explanations of the genesis, structures, and functions of their own religion which reinforce the *concealed* character of the historico-social dimension of their religious beliefs and practices.

Not that there is a deliberate attempt, "with malice aforethought," to conceal this dimension. (Or if there is, it has nothing to do with this particular sociological explanation.) What seems to happen is that the complex and conflictive nature of the social relationships in the midst of which beliefs and practices develop makes a sociological explanation of them difficult, whereas it facilitates the generation of spontaneous "theological" explanations of religious phenomena.

This key idea has its corollary: the self-interpretations put forward by religions cannot be admitted by sociology as an *explanation* of religious phenomena, but only as an *object* of the sociological analysis of religions.

The sociology of religions notes that, in similar social conditions, religions seemingly very different from one another behave similarly. Conversely, interpretation of the same creed or cult varies from age to age, from cultural ambient to cultural ambient, and from social group to social group. Certain constants appear in the comparative study of the development of different religious institutions. The sociology of religion notices that, often, the principles explicitly enunciated and pursued by the authorities or influential persons in a given religion are not followed in practice. What is more, sometimes such a religion appears actually to contribute, without its protagonists' being aware of it, to effects directly contrary to the intentions of its adherents.

It is as a result of these and similar data that the founders of the sociology of religions began to suspect that it is the complex, blind mechanisms of society that form, to a large extent and without the awareness of believers—indeed, even against their intentions—the motivations, organization, and functions of religious beliefs and practices. In other words, the place we occupy in the social system orients and impels us to think and act in a certain manner in the area of religion too—without our realizing it, and in spite of our intention to do just the opposite.

Marx, Weber, and Durkheim go even further. They assert that what the faithful generally suppose to be the sole motives of their conduct—which they think are within the structure of their church or sect—and what they insist are the social consequences of their life as believers, do *not* correspond to what really happens. Rather, in its ignorance of these social motivations, structures, and functions—an ignorance traceable to the complexity and opacity of society's functioning—the religious institution spontaneously produces an explanation of itself, in accordance with the traditions, intentions, and situation of its believers.

In a way, then, the sociology of religion begins with a suspicion and a lack of confidence. It begins with the *suspicion* that, behind the image that believers make of themselves, their history, their organization, and their aims, there lurks a network of social interaction very distinct from, and much more complex than, the believers' "self-image." Hence the sociology of religions entertains a *lack of confidence* in the spontaneous explanation shared by believers and their official representatives with regard to their beliefs, organization, and the ends they assure us these serve.

This suspicion and lack of confidence have nothing in common with the anticlerical moralism that thinks it finds "ulterior motives" and "secret plans" in religious preaching and practice. No, this suspicion and reserve typify the scientist, who thinks that the deeper explanation of social processes, including religious processes in their sociological dimension, are not to be found on the surface of phenomena, in the plain light of day, but below and behind the surface.

The sociologist is convinced that the hard work of dredging, searching, and penetrating is required in order to be in a position to work out an explanation of the structure and movement of society. In this hard work resides the task of the sociology of religion: to reconstruct the social dynamic behind the self-image of religious institutions. It does this by developing a satisfactory explanation of the traits of religious beliefs and practices in their specific social context.

Religious Phenomena, Social Phenomena

Inasmuch as the objective of sociology is to "explain the social by the social," what will be the objective of the sociology of religions? It will be to explain religions insofar as they are social phenomena, based on the social context within which each religion has evolved. But is this not some kind of profanation? By no means. It is simply the application of the scientific method—an attempt to explain scientifically whatever can be explained scientifically—without renouncing the method even when something seems difficult to explain from its viewpoint. And in spite of the hesitation and complaints of many believers, the sociology of religion has gradually managed to win the "right" to pursue its specific objective.

Sociology is not a matter of "dogma," as if perchance sociologists of religion maintained that a religion could be explained only and exclusively, in its totality, by the sociological method. No, there are those who make this claim, but for me the sociological objective in the area of religions is a matter of *trying out* a sociological explanation of religious phenomena, and seeing how far it is feasible and useful. Nor should the attempt be abandoned at the first appearance of difficulties and obstacles.

This is called "methodological materialism" in the social sciences: the provisory bracketing off of the metasocial—the supernatural, in this particular case—in order to attempt to give a *sociological* explanation—here, of religious beliefs and rites, whose internal reference is to the supernatural and metasocial. This method is also termed the "methodical atheism" of the sciences: the provisory suspension of the investigator's personal opinions on the existence and activity of supernatural beings, in order to prevent such opinions from penetrating scientific research as "criteria," and to admit such opinions in the course of scientific research only as *objects* of scientific analysis. After all, is this not how any good church historian examines and attempts to explain the church—however devoted he or she may be to the doctrines and practice of the church whose history is being investigated and explained?

Briefly and simply, to do sociology of religion is to look at and study all religions (equally) as social phenomena. That is, the sociology of religions is the study of religions as phenomena that are socially *produced*, socially *situated* and *limited*, socially *orientated* and *structured*, and have an *influence* upon the society in which they find themselves. And therefore in order to do sociology of religions it is necessary to render oneself capable (however provisionally and fictitiously—that is, purely methodologically) of putting one's own religious beliefs and preferences in parentheses, in suspension.

A difficult task! But—beyond doubt—one that is *possible*. And it may be one that will do future believers more good than we present believers tend to think.

Chapter Four

IS THERE A LATIN AMERICAN SOCIOLOGY OF RELIGIONS?

Latin America is generally considered to be Catholic, for the most part. In fact, statistically speaking, there are more baptized Catholics in Latin America than in any other continent. Historically, the subjugation of this continent by the empires of Spain and Portugal was accompanied by the setting up of Catholicism as *the* official religion. There is no need to consult a scientific study to be convinced that the cultural consequences of this process bear at least one indisputable trait: in the Latin American religious field, Catholicism is the predominant religion.

The indigenous cults of this continent have not totally disappeared, and perhaps they even harbor a potential that will permit them to spring up once more and blossom in the future. But at least for now, these cults are truncated, fragmented, and subjected to a culture that is predominantly marked by Catholicism. The same is to be said of the African cults, handed down by the black slaves of days gone by. The case is somewhat different with the various Protestant denominations and other religious bodies of non-Latin American origin. In spite of their minority and subordinate status, they are perhaps somewhat better rooted now, in the locales where they have been established, than are the novel cults of recent implantation: nonmainline religious sects that have arrived among us in the last twenty years—Mormons, Gnostics, Children of God, Hare Krishna, and others.

It is true that native, African, and Christian traditions are often mixed in Latin America, in variable proportions and with different results, yielding a syncretistic religious phenomenon. But even this syncretism is generally subordinated to a large extent, directly or indirectly, to Catholicism.

Latin American Catholicism is a "dependent" Catholicism. Even at a distance of some five hundred years from the arrival of Christopher Columbus on our shores, the relationship of the Latin American Catholic Church with the Vatican and with the Spanish Catholic Church is one of extreme subordination. Our priests, brothers, and sisters, when they are not trained in Europe, are educated by programs, textbooks, and teachers of the Old World pattern. Only in the past decade—since the CELAM meeting in Medellín and

20

the appearance of a theology of liberation—has one been able to discern the outlines of an authentically Latin American thought process within the Catholicism of our continent.

The vast majority of the religious orders at work in Latin America are of European origin. Their generalates, where vital decisions affecting their members worldwide are taken, are in Europe. A great part of our clergy is imported; Venezuela is the most extreme case, with 84 percent of its clergy foreign-born, mostly European, and largely Spanish. Latin American Catholicism, then, today still, is more European than Latin American, in its origin, in its clergy, in its background and schooling, and in its orientation.

These traits of the Latin American religious world—those of a Catholicism that is *predominant and dependent*—have without a doubt left their mark on the sociology of religion as it has developed on our continent until very recently.

Sociology in and of Latin America

Who has been "doing sociology" in Latin America? This question is a very easy one to answer. Analyses of the impact of Latin American social processes in the religious field, and vice versa, along with research into the sociological traits of religion, have until now been solicited, orientated, financed, developed, published, and utilized mainly by organs of the Catholic Church. And inasmuch as the sociology of religions is a discipline of European origin, it has been mainly European Catholic sociologists (clergymen, largely) who have been most concerned to acquire a knowledge of our socio-religious reality.[26]

Why and to what purpose has sociology been done in Latin America? Our continent has undergone a series of technological, economic, political, military, educational, hygienic, demographic, spatial, communicational, and cultural transformations throughout the course of this present century. These profound transformations have had marked repercussions on agricultural and industrial production, and the relationships between them; hence, on the habitat, employment, expectations, and mentality of the population of the continent, its family and community structures, and so on. This whole complexus of changes has placed the Catholic Church in Latin America within a network of new problems, unforeseen interrelationships, and unfamiliar pressures.[27] Accustomed as it is to a traditional, almost immobile, society, adopting changes very slowly, centered on agriculture, crafts, and small business, based on family units, the church now sees itself suddenly overwhelmed —and often marginalized—by the processes of urbanization and industrialization, and by the phenomenon of the mass migration and proletarianization of rural populations.

Faced with this battery of problems, church institutions have made an effort to understand what is happening, where society is going, and how the church can adapt to this new type of society in order to survive in the midst of its changes. This complex situation—which in and of itself would be worthy of sociological analysis—became an incentive to take up the tools that European Catholicism had used in analogous circumstances. Thus Latin American Catholicism began to make use of the sociology of religion.

Because these unexpected new social processes posed problems and occasioned conflicts for which the church felt ill prepared, certain groups of the clergy sought in its European matrix the instrumentation that would help them understand what was happening in Latin America in the nineteen-fifties. They sought it in the European sociology of Catholic scholars— Lebras, Pin, Houtart, Remy, Carrier, Boulard, and others.

Why were they seeking to understand the crisis? Mainly in order to find a way out of it. They were by no means calling into question the social processes taking place in Latin America. The church was doing what *any* social institution spontaneously tends to do when confronted with a major crisis: try to find the means to survive, to endure, and to perpetuate itself, while preserving, as fully as possible, the power it enjoyed before the crisis. Thus the sociology of religions enters Latin America as a means by which the Catholic Church is attempting to understand the changes in Latin American society and meet them. "Thus sociology becomes a weapon of pastoral theology and practice"[28]—of a *specific* pastoral theology and practice: that of institutional survival in an atmosphere of resignation to societal change.

How, then, has the sociology of religions been done in Latin America? First and foremost, from the viewpoint of the immediate interests of the church as a social institution. The problem posed has not been so much why Latin America is undergoing these transformations, who benefits from them, and what the long-term outlook of these transformations is for the population of the continent. Instead, these societal changes are accepted by the church as a *fait accompli*, almost as a natural event. On occasion there have been Catholic leaders who see in these changes a welcome "verdict of history," with which the church should cooperate. But even here the problem the church poses to itself is mainly that of how such transformations directly affect the ecclesiastical institution, and what to do to assure a "realistic" minimum of damage to the institution and a maximum preservation of its traditional status.

Secondly, the sociology of religion is done—in Latin America—with a European (Italo-Iberian) model of what the church should be.[29] Armed with such a model, one studies the Latin American situation and tries to see where, how, and how much the situation has departed from the model. Such an approach to reality results almost at once in decisions to conform church life (parochial or diocesan situations) to this European model. Only very seldom is the possibility entertained of making this "European model of the church" itself an object of analysis, in order to analyze *its* historical origins, viability, and possible future social functions.

In sum, the sociology of religions that has been done in Latin America by the Catholic Church has been *adaptive* (we would almost say "conservative" with regard to the church, and "submissive" with regard to social changes), *clerical* (that is, mainly concerned with the preservation of the ecclesiastical institution), and *Eurocentric* (based on the European model of what the church "ought to be").[30]

Latin America, thus, since the nineteen-fifties, has seen the development of one particular sociology of religion. This sociology of religion has consisted mainly of a "sociography"[31] of the inadequacies of the Latin American church as measured against the Italo-Iberian model of church. Developed almost entirely by the church-institution and European clerics, such a "sociology of religions" was thought of, by and large, as an "arm of the pastoral ministry." It was intended to help pinpoint the inadequacies in the Latin American church, with a view to bringing it into alignment with the European model of the church. It was meant to help adapt church structures to a Latin America recognized as undergoing changes—but those changes are almost never questioned.

Deficiencies of Latin American Sociography

The answer to the question of whether or not there is a Latin American sociology of religion is: yes and no. We could answer *yes*, inasmuch as for nearly a quarter of a century now sociological studies have been under way on the various religions of Latin America. These investigations have contributed a research experience and a mass of information that will be indispensable for a scientific knowledge of religious dynamics in Latin American societies. In this sense, then, yes, there *does* exist a Latin American sociology of religions —just getting under way.

But, in parallel fashion, we could answer *no*. The sociology that has been done to date has been mainly a *sociography*—a description of isolated religious phenomena—rather than a *sociology* of macrosocial processes. It is true that this sociography has been done *about* Latin America, but it has not been done from a Latin American perspective. It has been done from a European perspective. Nor has it been done from the viewpoint of the Latin American peoples and their common interests, but from the viewpoint of the particular interests of the Catholic ecclesiastical institution.

Furthermore, this sociography, rather than being concerned with religions in Latin America, has focused on the degree of inadequacy of Latin American popular practice of religion as measured against an Italo-Iberian paradigm of church. Finally, what little has been done, with its scant resources and inadequate publication, has been discontinuous, scattered, and sporadic. For all these reasons, then, we can say that an authentic Latin American sociology of religion has *not* yet come into existence.

What, then, would an "authentic" Latin American sociology of religion be? Is the sociology that is being done "bad" sociology?

Chapter Five

NAIVE SPONTANEITY OR AUTOCRITICAL PARTIALITY?

The sociology of religions that has been done in Latin America until now has been a sociology that approaches its object—Latin American religions— *naively.*

This sociology does not ask itself, for instance, whether the development model currently prevailing in Latin America is the only viable one, or whether on the contrary there are other alternatives. This sociology has not asked itself what groups or interests control the current orientation of Latin American development. This sociology has not posed the question of what the medium- and long-range consequences of this style of development will be for the majority of Latin Americans, for their family and local organization, for their culture and way of life, for their ecological environment and their bio-psycho-social health and well-being. Instead—and this is why we call it naive—this sociology has simply verified and accepted the type of development that guides the destinies of our continent today almost as if it were an inevitable fact of nature.

We can say, then—to use an explanatory metaphor—that our sociology of religion has been myopic. It has been a sociology situating itself within the process of Latin American development without attempting to look beyond the data immediately given. It takes its seat in the audience of Latin American history with a short-term, unmediated vision. It is characterized, then, by the absence of an investigation into the genesis, deeper implications, goals, fundamental orientations, power centers, and possible alternatives of our prevailing model of development.

Then again, the sociology of religion being done in Latin America has often been markedly *spontaneous* in nature.

Spontaneous? Yes, in the sense that this sociology has arisen from within the Catholic Church as it is, without a scientific analysis of that church in its history, its structuring, its social functioning, and the influence exercised upon the organization and orientation of the church itself by the prevailing power centers. Latin American sociology of religions arose as a defensive reaction of the ecclesiastical institution against the assaults of the process of development prevailing in Latin America. This is why we term it "spontaneous."

The ecclesiastical institutions that have produced and utilized the greater part of the sociological research into Latin American religion have done so without posing either themselves or their socio-political ambient as the *object* of a thorough-going analysis. On the contrary, these institutions have set out from a point of departure in themselves and their socio-political ambient as if these were *unquestionable data*. They have been doing religious sociology without examining themselves sociologically, without calling themselves into question, without interrogating themselves scientifically about the interests that the church has in fact served, is serving now, and could serve, as the social institution that it is.

In this sense too we could label our Latin American tradition of the sociology of religions as myopic. It is myopic in the sense that it has accepted the church (the institution that produced this sociology) basically as it is. At most it has only made some effort to analyze the "manner" in which the church's message is expressed, in order to determine whether it is "efficacious," and if it is not, to introduce changes that would permit it to "maximalize" this "efficacity"—which very rarely means anything beyond adaptation to the prevailing model of development. The problem of "efficacity" has practically never been examined in depth; it has always been understood in a superficial and immediate sense.

In its myopia, this sociology has never permitted itself to pose the crucial and decisive problem of the relationship between the church (in its dimension as social institution) and society in its totality—what interests (economic, political, military, and so on), what social guises, and what model of development the ecclesiastical institution is serving (whether it knows it or not), and how, and why. Nor has it questioned itself about viable alternatives that this church could have apart from the Italo-Iberian model.

In sum—and taking another viewpoint—we could suggest that Latin American ecclesiastical institutions, predominantly Catholic and very dependent, have been spontaneously and naively producing a sociology of religion to their own image and likeness. They have produced a sociology that is naively dependent and spontaneously Catholic.

Myopia vs. Hyperopia

Perhaps what we have said in these last pages is too heavily laden with adjectives—emotionally negative adjectives. Calling the prevailing sociological orientation "naive, dependent, myopic, and superficial" could be rather unscientific—and, above all, could be of too little help in objectively evaluating our sociological tradition. Perhaps we have ourselves been guilty of "spontaneity, naivety, myopia, and superficiality." And indeed it is by no means easy to do sociology of religions without allowing the tastes, aversions, preferences, values, theological and political positions, and so on, that originally aroused our interest in this discipline, to interpose themselves in the course of our work.

Let us admit, then—thereby qualifying somewhat our indictment of our Latin American sociological tradition—that a sociology of religions could hardly have arisen in Latin America in any other way than that in which in fact it did arise. This discipline could hardly have come to our shores except from the part of the church, as a reaction to the problems of urban-industrial capitalistic development, based on a European viewpoint, and in view of adapting the church to this development in order to survive (without questioning either the development or the church).

In any case, this is how a sociology of religions has arisen in Latin America, whether we like it or not. Furthermore, the manner in which the sociology of religions has been done in Latin America until now is in a certain sense probably the "best" way it could have begun. What? After all we have said before, can we now say this? Yes, we have to. After all, among the traits that have characterized the Latin American sociological endeavor with respect to religion there are many whose results are positive, even indispensable, for a fruitful continuation of that same endeavor. We have sociographical information aplenty, we have acquired a fondness for observable data, we have constructed descriptive typologies based on statistically valid and reliable research techniques, we have set up meaningful correlations among empirically controllable sociological variables, and so on.

Let us recognize, then, our debt to tradition. If there is "myopia" in its penchant for immediate facts, at least this helps to avoid the other extreme of sociological "hyperopia"—the inability to see anything but alternatives, remote causes, ultimate consequences, and so on, in blissful disdain of anything like the real, concrete, immediate process of the sociologically relevant *facts* in the field of Latin American religion.

Let us recognize our debt to tradition. But let us by no means continue in this tradition without criticizing it or modifying it. Let us recognize that in all probability the sociology of religion could not have been born in Latin America in any other way. We must accept the fact of the traits of religious sociology in Latin America that has preceded us. We must also accept whatever is positive, appropriate, and indispensable in our socio-religious legacy south of the Rio Grande.

Once we have done all this, however, let us also reflect on the alternatives posed for the future course of our discipline. Let us thereupon define an orientation option that will permit us at one and the same time to escape traditional "myopia" without falling into a sociological "hyperopia." We must look for an option that will permit us to take our leave of one naivety without falling into the other. We must try to define an orientating option that will enable us to extricate ourselves from a "spontaneous sociology," but with the consciousness of not having a monopoly on *the* scientifically infallible method—an option that will show us how to flee an adaptive view without substituting a metaphysical utopiaism for it, an option that will help us abandon the tendency to use sociology as a defensive and immediate pastoral weapon without delivering ourselves up to a sort of anticlerical hypercriticism.

Epistemological Vigilance

In a word, we must develop an "epistemological vigilance." This will be a permanent, critical consciousness of the limits of our capacity to know reality, and of the "concealing and distorting" tendencies of this same capacity. Such an epistemological vigilance will allow us to preserve the successes tradition has scored without repeating its errors or committing worse ones.

What, then, do we propose? What alternative do we submit for consideration, in order to reorientate—to "authenticate"—contemporary Latin American sociology of religion?

To begin, I want to stress how vital it is to adopt a reflective attitude, one that is conscious of the powerful conditioning influence of the investigator's situation upon his or her definition of *what* should be investigated, *how* it should be investigated, and what *purpose* the investigation will in fact serve. In other words it is important to take cognizance of the fact that no analysis of society is neutral, impartial, "pure," or "objective" in the strict sense. On the contrary, *every* analysis of society seems to be strongly biased. But there can be no question of renouncing sociology just because sociology is obliged to carry out a study that will take sides—just as there can be no question of allowing oneself to be led spontaneously and naively by one's own personal side-taking in the study of social phenomena. By no means.

What is needed—it seems to me—is to *consciously* and *autocritically* assume and accept the biased view that is ours, that is each individual's. It is a matter of rendering our personal situation and attitude a conscious one, of seeing how this situation of ours colors our analysis of society, and of taking the appropriate means for preventing this situation from concealing from us (or distorting) those aspects of reality that are relevant for the feasible aims that we propose—consciously—to pursue.

Indeed, what we criticize in the traditional fashion of doing sociology of religions in Latin America is not that it has been side-taking. And it is not that it has been adaptive and dependent. What we basically criticize in this tradition—we would almost say, the only thing we criticize in it—is that it believed it was impartial. What we criticize is its lack of awareness of and concern with its partiality—with the factors that limit it and orientate it, with the interests that motivate it, with the ends that it in fact serves without knowing it and perhaps even without wishing it. I think that the reason for the complete failure of this traditional sociology of religions in its explicit intentions is, to an enormous extent, its ignorance of the real social conditions in which it developed.

If there is anything sociologists have to learn, in spite of all, from their discipline's founders, in order not to see their conscious intentions frustrated, it is precisely this: that the ends in fact served by a social activity depend much less on the intentions of those undertaking the activity than on the social conditions in which the activity is carried on.

For my part, I think that the traditional sociology of religions has contributed to its own failure to achieve its aims by believing that all one has to do in order to carry certain intentions into effect is to have them in mind. This sociology has attempted to penetrate the complex situation of the church in Latin American society without taking cognizance of how its own driving principle has led it in fact to be at the service of particular interests—at times, interests that have been opposed to those it explicitly intended to serve.

We do not have to repeat history. It is inevitable that we occupy a position in social processes, but it is possible to change one's position in those processes. Of course, to change that position it is necessary first to know it and appreciate it—to understand the position one occupies and defends. Then, one must determine which alternatives are really feasible, objectively viable.

Consequently, we propose for Latin America not an impartial sociology of religion, but a sociology that will be *conscious* of its inescapable partiality, and capable of accepting that partiality *autocritically*. These qualities will enable its practitioners to carry it efficaciously to its ultimate consequences, or to alter it efficaciously in line with an alternative that will be more viable and more in accord with the explicit interests of those claiming to do this sociology.

And yet even this will still not be enough. A sociology of religion can be done with a consciousness of its partiality, and with an ability to accept and assume it, and nevertheless allow the investigator to overlook (or falsely evaluate) aspects of reality that could be relevant to the attainment of the ends that he or she wishes to pursue.

Hence it is necessary for sociologists of religion, in taking cognizance of their specific partiality (that is, of their objective position in history, in society, and, where applicable, in the church; and of their subconscious conceptions and tacit value judgments concerning humanity, society, and religion) and of the manner in which this partiality orientates their analysis of reality, to concentrate on discovering those aspects of reality that this partiality systematically tends to conceal, undervalue, or distort.

In other words, we are urging a sociology of religion that is not simply conscious of its partiality, but simultaneously committed to and involved in a *deliberate and ongoing self-critique* with respect to the obstacles to a knowledge of reality that its particular, partial position will unavoidably set up. In this it will differ from the sociology of religions practiced throughout the greater part of our tradition until now, in which these characteristics were lacking.

By way of synthesis: over against the naive spontaneity of Latin American sociological tradition with respect to the question of religions in society, we propose a sociology of religions that will be (1) conscious of its partiality, and (2) autocritical.

This proposal, in this rather abstract formulation, leaves the door open to a broad spectrum of theoretical orientations that not only do not agree, but are in conflict with one another. And there is no way for us to close this door. But the spectrum narrows as we come down to the concrete level of the positions objectively in conflict today in the social structure and religious field of Latin America. For it is not the history of philosophy which defines ultimately the positions toward which we shall unavoidably show a partiality, whether we are aware of it or not. It is only on the basis of the social conflicts being waged in the immediate history of Latin America that socially feasible positions can be defined. They are what make our partiality—spontaneous or self-critical, naive or conscious—inevitable. Ultimately (sociologically speaking), the partiality of a Latin American sociology of religions can take shape only vis-à-vis the real elements (and their feasible alternatives) objectively in conflict in Latin American society—whether we know it or not, and whether we like it or not.

This is the premise (doubtless open to attack, but defensible, and not yet refuted) upon which I base my own personal sociological option. It is only *one among many* possible options for a consciously partial and autocritical analysis of religions in Latin America.

Chapter Six

CRITICO-POLITICAL SOCIOLOGY OF RELIGION BASED ON THE LATIN AMERICAN PRAXIS OF LIBERATION

As we have said, various sociological options seem to be possible today in Latin America for the study of the religious phenomena of our continent in their dimension as part of our social dynamic.

We start with the premise that every sociological option is—whether we know it or not—an option taken in partiality. And we clearly assert that the particular partiality of any Latin American sociology of religion will be a function of the groups actually in conflict in the conduct of Latin American society.

To be sure, one could counterbalance this premise with a different, opposed, point of departure. For example, there are those who would argue that religious sociology is a matter of studying socio-religious reality objectively and exhaustively without any partiality at all. But taking up this position will be possible and easy in direct proportion to the particular sociologist's distancing from, or vantage point outside, Latin America, and the purity of his or her interest simply to know "what is happening there."

For example, a Japanese sociologist who has won a grant for a research project in Brazilian spiritism will find it relatively easy to maintain such an "objectivizing" position, inasmuch as he or she is materially and spiritually "disconnected" from the economic, social, political, and religious conflicts taking place on this continent. To such a sociologist, all this "partiality" in sociology can appear as just so much nonsense. But such a sociologist will not be able (nor would a Latin American sociologist either) to study all the macrosocial religious phenomena, or analyze all the interrelationships of those they study, or capture from all possible points of view the interrelationships they analyze, or, finally, make use of all the techniques appropriate for the viewpoints they assume.

Why not? Simply because life is not long enough, nor are the resources at their disposition sufficiently abundant. Then what will this Japanese sociologist, like any Latin American sociologist, do? He or she will have to end by opting for particular areas of study, seeking a certain type of interrelationships, analyzing them from a few select viewpoints and selecting among available and appropriate techniques.

Of course, such a process of *selection* implies at the same time a process of *exclusion*. Many areas of possible study, an enormous number of interrelationships, various feasible viewpoints, and a great part of the available techniques for the investigation and processing of pertinent data will necessarily be thrust aside, at least provisionally.

Furthermore, the Japanese sociologist will have to consciously or unconsciously make *decisions*—decisions as to form and language, decisions as to when, where, with whom, and in what circumstances he or she will be developing the investigation and presenting its results. Again he or she will have to opt for—choose—and exclude a significant number of viable alternatives. Why? Again, because he or she will have neither the time nor the resources to permit the pursuit of all feasible alternatives.

And finally, this whole complexus of choices and exclusions will delimit and orientate the *probable social functions* of our Japanese sociologist's investigation. Consciously or not, and intentionally or not, the taking of all these decisions will facilitate certain social uses the investigation will have, and not facilitate others. These decisions will make it easy for some groups to use the investigation and hard for others. It will favor one development policy, and not another.

Coherent, Explicit, Self-Critical Partiality

When all is said and done, this process of options, choices, decisions, selections, and exclusions will amount to a certain *partiality*. Its degree of *coherence* will be proportioned to the *social conditions* in which the researcher develops the work, and to the *degree of consciousness* with which the researcher makes explicit and assumes the unavoidable partiality.

What do we mean by "coherence"? We speak of a position of partiality in sociology as coherent when there is a certain agreement or consonance, a relative adequation, a relative absence of contradiction, between (1) the societal objectives explicitly taken up by the researcher (whether to be achieved or to be avoided), and (2) the fields of investigation, the interrelationships analyzed, the viewpoints accepted, the techniques adopted (and, especially, those rejected), the form, the language, and the groups with and by which the researcher develops and presents the investigation.

The achievement of such a coherence, which is probably never total, will be easier if the societal objectives explicitly taken up by researchers are identical with the predominant societal orientations of their ambient. The attainment of this coherence will be more difficult, on the other hand, for researchers who are "against the system." They will have to swim against the current.

On the contrary, we say that a nonimpartial position in sociology is "incoherent" when this agreement, this relative adequation between the societal objectives the sociologist explicitly takes up and the various levels of sociological investigation that we have differentiated above, is not in evidence. *Incoherence*, then, will mark the case of a systematic and persistent inadequation, disagreement, and contradiction between explicitly espoused societal objectives on the one hand, and on the other the characteristics of the research project. Obviously a certain incoherence will be present in any sociological investigation. Only social conditions and the degree of the sociologist's autocritical consciousness will determine if such incoherence is merely marginal, or indissolubly a part of the overall objective, in each concrete case.

The social conditions and the degree of consciousness in which the sociology of religions has until now been developed in Latin America have invested its inescapable partiality with a high degree of incoherence. Indeed, the area in which it has been practiced, the vision animating it, the viewpoints explicitly assumed and the underlying problematic defining it, the social interests that it has sought to serve, and the conception of society that has orientated it, are so incongruent and incompatible among themselves that this sociological tradition can be qualified only as incoherent. But like its other traits, it seems to us, the incoherence of this sociology is sociologically explicable.

Indeed, sociology of religions as done in Latin America until now has been done from a point of departure in a religious institution—the Catholic Church—whose structural situation on this continent is, from many points of view, overwhelmingly ambiguous. It is present and active in Latin America— but with a history, a mentality, and an organization still anchored in Europe. And it is intimately bound up with the Latin American masses—but significantly subjected to and influenced by that continent's governments and powerful classes. It is uncomfortable with certain consequences, for itself and the major part of its audience, issuing from the new course set by Latin American nations, to be sure. But it is prevented from transcending a conciliatory view of social conflicts and an elitist and reformist outlook on social change. In a situation such as has marked the Catholic Church in Latin America, it has been practically impossible for it to produce a sociology of religions that would be conscious, autocritical, and coherently biased.

What the Latin American Catholic Church has produced has been, to my way of thinking, a sociology of religion that has indeed been partial, but also spontaneous, incoherent, and naive.

Meanwhile, the parties currently in conflict in Latin America, as well as the alternatives that each of them proposes, are being defined with greater and greater clarity. In a certain sense, this process both demands and facilitates the development of a greater clarity and coherence in the partiality of the options taken in Latin American sociological analysis. As this process develops at the societal level, there appear, crystalize, grow, and come into mutual confrontation in its midst, various tendencies more or less clearly linked to various socio-political options in conflict on that level. Some, such as the "Tradition, Family, and Property" movement, defend tooth and nail the prevailing social order. Others, such as the "theology of liberation" and "Christians for Socialism," maintain a commitment to a revolutionary option linked to the interests of the populous sectors of the continent. And between them there is a tendency—a widely shared and predominant one, it would seem—that oscillates between reformist positions and claims of political neutrality.

Thus, social conditions and the degree of consciousness developing in Latin America—which have their repercussions on the Latin American Catholic Church—raise the possibility, and likewise the demand, for sociology to take a position whose partiality is coherent and conscious, and not just a position whose partiality is naive, spontaneous, and incoherent.

For our part, from among the several possible options in partiality, we have taken that of working in a Latin American sociology of religions from a conscious, coherent, and autocritical viewpoint, in partiality with the struggles of Latin America's oppressed sectors for their self-liberation, and in pursuit of a self-governing socialist society.[32]

By no means do we pretend that this is the only viable option. It is but one among many. Nor do we even defend it as the best of all possible options. From the viewpoint of the long-range interests of the urban and rural working classes and the marginalized of this continent it will perhaps eventuate as the best option (for them). Perhaps. But even this remains to be seen. Then too, on the contrary, from other viewpoints, this could be an unsuitable option, perhaps the worst of all. Perhaps. But this, too, remains to be seen.

What we are claiming here is that this option is—at the very least—a *viable* and *legitimate* one. Of course, it could be objected that the option we have summarily characterized as our own is not a properly sociological option at all, but an ideologico-political one. For that very reason—according to the objection—instead of contributing to a scientific analysis of society and religion, it would vitiate *a priori* any study undertaken on its basis.

An extended discussion of the complex and inescapable relationships between political ideology and social science[33] would be out of place in this work, and we shall not embark upon it. What we shall do is make clear that, indeed, we are taking our point of departure from an "ideologico-political" option. And we claim that this point of departure is a viable and legitimate one for outlining the orientation of a sociological analysis.

We do not admit to introducing a novelty. As we have seen, every sociological option—willy-nilly—is taken in partiality, and this partiality inescapably partakes, in one way or another—consciously or not, coherently or not, autocritically or not—of an ideologico-political character. What may be somewhat novel in our option, in the Latin American tradition in sociology of religion, is only our earnest concern that the ideologico-political partiality characterizing the point of departure of our investigation of the development of religions in Latin American society be *explicit, coherent,* and *autocritical.*

As for vitiating the sociological analysis orientated by our option, this is an ongoing danger for any option.[34] We scarcely think the danger will be greater simply because the option is explicit. On the contrary, we are convinced that a consciousness of the interests that inspire a research project is extraordinarily helpful, precisely for the purpose of preventing such interests from guiding analysis blindly. Instead, we hold, such consciousness helps us foresee and control the concealing and distorting effect of these interests.

Let us now clearly define, once and for all, what this option that we have taken consists in—concretely—and what traits it implies on the level of the orientation of the sociological approach to religious phenomena.

A Latin American Sociology . . .

First, our option is for a critical *Latin American* sociology of religions.

The *locus* we have chosen from which to do sociology of religions is Latin America. Inasmuch as our effort intends to be properly a Latin American one, we refuse to see ourselves with the eyes of an outsider. We reject the imposition of a European (or North American) model of what Latin America "ought to be" socially and religiously.

We intend to do a sociology of Latin America such as it in fact is: *dependent.*[35] But, because our sociology seeks to be a critical one, we accept this dependency only as a contingent fact, not as an irrevocable fact. On the contrary, we take our point of departure in the *possibility* of an independent, autonomous Latin America. From the double viewpoint of this fact and this possibility, our sociological examination will be directed toward those socioreligious processes that appear to contribute to and reinforce dependence, and those others that, by contrast, appear to tend to debilitate dependency and form the basis of a Latin American identity and autonomy.

. . . of the Oppressed . . .

Secondly, our option is for a critical sociology of religions from a point of departure in the praxis of the *oppressed.*

The social sector in Latin America with which we identify in order to do sociology of religions from a point of departure in their situation is that of the urban and rural working classes and the marginalized. Hence we refuse to look at ourselves with elitist eyes,[36] and we reject any *a priori* conception of social and religious reality as the harmonious enterprise of groups that by nature are "diverse but complementary." We seek to do a sociology of Latin American peoples such as we see them to be in fact: *oppressed.*

But, once again, inasmuch as our sociology intends to be critical, we recognize in this oppression only a fundamental datum, not a perpetual reality. On the contrary, we presuppose the *possibility* of a Latin America without oppression—with neither oppressors nor oppressed. From the perspective of this datum and this possibility, our sociological examination will prefer an orientation toward those socio-religious processes that appear to have contributed to the generation and reinforcement of the situation of oppression, as also, complementarily, toward those other socio-religious processes that seem to debilitate relationships of oppression and contribute to the development of the popular classes as autonomous and combative classes.

. . . based on the struggles for Liberation . . .

Thirdly, we make our option for a critical sociology of religions from a point of departure in the *praxis of the liberation* of the oppressed.

The *socio-political process* from whose standpoint we propose to do sociology of religions is the struggle of the oppressed against their oppression, their struggle for self-liberation. Consequently we refuse to see ourselves through a conservative lens. And we reject the social and religious notion that society is essentially in equilibrium, and only incidentally or accidentally conflictive. We seek to do a sociology of Latin American peoples as they truly are: *in conflict.*

But, again, because our sociology seeks to be a critical one, we perceive in this conflict only a key aspect of our reality, and not the only and eternal reality. On the contrary, we think there exists the *possibility*, by way of the struggles of the oppressed against oppression, of the rise of a Latin America that would be characterized by a comradely community of justice.

Thus, from the perspective of this conflictive aspect of reality, and this possibility, our sociological examination will be directed toward the socio-religious processes that seem to present an obstacle to the development of the consciousness, the alliances, the organization, and the struggles of the oppressed classes in their efforts against oppression. It will as well be directed toward those other socio-religious processes that, by contrast, appear to contribute to the development of such consciousness, alliances, organization, and struggles.

. . . toward Socialism

Finally, we make our option for a critical sociology of religions from a point of departure in the struggles of the oppressed for a self-directing Latin American *socialism.*

The *utopian*[37] *alternative*, within whose vision we place ourselves in order to do sociology of religions from a point of departure in its "desirable possibility," is that of a self-governing—self-directing and self-managing—Latin American socialism.[38] Hence we refuse to see ourselves through the eyes of the industrialized nations. And we reject the social and religious alternative of capitalism as the only model of our development.

We seek to do a sociology of Latin American society such as it is today:

capitalistic. But, inasmuch as our sociology intends to be critical, we understand that although capitalism has been the prevailing development model in Latin America throughout this century, it need not necessarily continue to control our destinies into the next century. On the contrary, we think there is the objective *possibility* of a socialist development of this continent.

Hence, working from this prevailing model and this objective possibility, we shall direct our sociological examination toward the socio-religious processes that appear to hold back the subjective intention and objective realization of the socialist alternative in Latin America. And we shall as well direct it toward those other processes that, on the contrary, seem to contribute to the implantation and realization of this alternative on our continent.

It is evident that the particular "option in partiality" that we have taken will tend to focus our gaze on some social relationships rather than on others. And it will tend to make us ask certain questions rather than others, incline us to examine the validity of certain hypotheses, adopt determinate viewpoints, and so on. And we shall yield to these tendencies, for we think that it is these problems (rather than others) which, in view of the interests with which we identify, are in most urgent need of delimitation and elucidation.

We concentrate upon these problems, then, not because we think that they are "objectively" the only problems of a Latin American sociology of religions, and not even because we see them as the most important or urgent problems, "in themselves." There will certainly be other problems, which will be provisionally excluded from our perspective. Only a self-critical sociological reflection, carried out in the midst of the praxis in which we are participants, will tell us, afterward, whether it will then be appropriate to include these other problems, excluded for the present, and whether it will be advantageous to adopt perspectives we have provisionally bracketed from consideration.

Thus, then, to conclude, what we propose is to construct a critico-political sociology of religions working from the *Latin American praxis of the socialist self-liberation of the oppressed*. This is a sociology that will keep a watchful eye on its own coherence and maintain an autocritical consciousness of its partiality.

We call this sociology *critico-political* for two reasons. First, because it seeks to be a sociology that does not accept reality as something given once and for all. It holds that our society contains within itself the objective possibility of one day—by our common endeavor—becoming a radically different society, one altogether distinct from what it has been our lot to live, suffer, study, and attempt to transform. By the same token, because it does not set up its own points of departure as dogma, but is born of a consciousness of its limits (being incomplete, provisional, partial in the sense of side-taking, and conjectural), it incorporates the insight that, by reason of these limits, it will be necessary and advantageous—in the near future—for it to modify itself in order to enhance its possibilities of service to the alternative for which it was originally undertaken.

Secondly, because this sociology sees contemporary Latin American society as a contradictory class structure, heterogeneous in its degrees of power. Among these classes a struggle is being waged, on the part of some, to preserve an acquired power-of-oppression ("reproduction"), and, on the part of the others, to increase their power to do away with this oppression by producing a different society ("production"). This is a struggle for the direction and management of society, carried out and expressed on different levels, in different degrees, and in different forms, permeating and having significant repercussions on all dimensions of Latin American life.

In view of all this, the problem of a Latin American sociology of religion begins to acquire its specificity, its own particularity. Our endeavor in the chapters that follow will be to propose *a set of problems, questions, perspectives, hypotheses, and concepts* intended to cover a single aspect of the task that we have just defined and delimited. We might call this aspect the "theoretical framework" of our particular Latin American sociology of religion.[39]

In what follows, then, we shall attempt to present a *provisional sketch, theoretical in character, for the analysis of the interrelationships between the religious field and the complexus of social conflicts in Latin America.*

PART II

Religion as a Product of Social Conflicts

The relationships between the "religious field"[40] and the whole complexus of social conflicts in Latin American societies can be studied under a number of aspects. In Part II we shall concentrate on just one of these aspects: the profound influence that social structure, and especially the conflicts inherent in social structure, exert on the religious field. In other words we shall examine the religious field as a *product* of social conflict.

But let us keep in mind that this is only *one* of the relationships between the religious field and social conflicts. In Parts III and IV, we shall study other relationships—distinct but complementary—between the religious field and society. To reduce religion simply to its character as a product of social conflicts would be to rob it of all its specificity.[41] But totally to ignore this aspect of the study of religion would prevent us from understanding a great part of the social reality of religion.[42]

In other words, what we are about to say in Part II will acquire its deepest meaning only to the extent that we place it in relationship with what we shall be asserting in Parts III and IV—and indeed in relationship with other, non-sociological, dimensions of religion to which we shall not even be referring in this work.

This study—may we be permitted to emphasize again—by no means pretends to exhaust the reality of religion. It seeks only to present a sociological introduction to the study of the relationships of the religious field with the conflicts being waged for the governance of society, especially in Latin America as it approaches the end of the twentieth century.

Chapter Seven

RELIGION IN SOCIETY

No religion exists in a vacuum. Every religion, any religion, no matter what we may understand by "religion," is a *situated* reality—situated in a specific human context, a concrete and determined geographical space, historical moment, and social milieu. Every religion is, in each concrete case, always the religion of these or those determinate human beings. A religion that would not be the religion of determinate human beings would be nonexistent, purely a phantasm of the imagination.

Real religions are always religions of concrete human beings. But concrete human beings sharing the same religion—any religion—are beings of flesh and blood. All have their determinate sex, determinate age, specific background and condition (family, cultural, economic, social, political, and so on), individual biography, individual hopes and expectations, and particular problems and interests.

Furthermore, human beings sharing a religion—any religion—are persons who not only believe and practice their religion, but who also feel hunger and seek food, feel the cold and try to find shelter, feel the desire for company and affection and pursue the satisfaction of this desire, feel fatigue and look for repose, perceive danger and flee it or face it, feel confusion and strive to explain the things that confuse them. Thus, human beings sharing a religion—any religion—are individuals who share not only these or those beliefs and religious rites, but also a certain way of producing, preparing, apportioning, and eating food, a particular way of constructing shelters, dwellings, a way of communicating among themselves (including, among other things, a language of their own), a particular form of social organization, of structuring their families and the relationships among family members, a way of distinguishing the useful from the futile, the good from the bad, the beautiful from the ugly, the just from the unjust, the logical from the absurd, the obligatory from the unacceptable.

In other words, human beings sharing a religion—any religion—share at the same time a collective life of multiple other dimensions—economic, affective, familial, linguistic, political, military, cultural, and so on. And these dimensions are closely linked among themselves. They all overlap, they are interrelated.

41

Thus, religion is not a watertight compartment isolated and held incommunicado from the other dimensions of the common life of its adherents. Quite the contrary, the concrete religion that determinate human beings share within their specific form of social organization is closely linked and interrelated with the rest of their social life, with all the other dimensions of the life of their community. A concrete religion is *situated* in a particular social context.

However long its history, however broad its extent throughout the world, whatever its internal cohesiveness, however jealous its efforts to preserve continuity with its origins, any religion—whatever religion it may be—has existence only insofar as it is *situated* in a particular social context. The only religions outside a determinate society are the extinct ones—the ones belonging to humanity's past. (Of course, even extinct religions, when they were alive, existed in specific social contexts. They were *socially situated*.)

At first sight, the assertion that every religion is socially situated in a particular context might seem rather banal and inconsequential. Let us delve a little deeper into the sociological content of this assertion.

The assertion that a religion is a reality *socially situated* in a particular context implies, from our sociological viewpoint, the following. The members of a religion—those who act in any way within that religion, those who "practice" that religion—do *not* move about within an infinite set of simultaneous alternatives for thinking, expressing, or practicing their religion. By no means. Further, the finite alternatives they have available for conceiving, expressing, or practicing their religion are not all equivalent alternatives. Quite the contrary, the set of alternatives (for thinking, verbalizing, and practicing their religion) at the disposition of the leaders and members of any religion—no matter how large a religion it may be—is a *finite* set of alternatives—which, furthermore (and even if its members are unaware of it), are each possible *to a different degree*, and with different implications.

Thus the first thing we must stress when we say that every religion is a socially situated reality is that this religion does not work with infinite, limitless "instruments," either in number or in kind. No, it operates, in every concrete case, with the *instruments that are socially available* in the context in which that religion is alive.

For example, it works with a particular language (whose vocabulary and meanings are limited), determinate natural resources, a specific population, and a limited set of means of production, distribution, exchange, consumption, and so forth. These instruments, with which the beings who form each society come into contact and with which they speak, produce, eat, and find shelter, are limited instruments, in quantity as well as in effective potential. But these are the only instruments with which a religion has to function—limited instruments of communication, production, and reproduction. And this limitation—in their number and in their characteristics—of the only instruments that any religion can have in any given case, *limits*, in turn, the potential for activity that any religion has within its particular society.

Hence when we say that every religion is a socially situated reality, we mean that each religion's activity is *limited* by the social context in which it operates. That is, its alternatives for activity (for thinking, speaking, and practicing its religious message) are *limited* by that context (independently of any consciousness of this, or intentions to this effect, on the part of the members of the religion).

But secondly, when we say that every religion is a socially situated reality, we are saying something else as well, something even more complex and important. We mean that no religion works with a "social material" that is shapeless, plastic, and susceptible of any modification at all. No, a religion always operates in a society already structured[43] in a particular manner.

For example, the language spoken there is a particular structure. So is a specific economic system, a particular type of family relationships, a specific political organization, a specific manner of dressing and eating, a definite set of mores and customs, and so on. This whole series of established customs determines, in each specific society, what is normal and what is abnormal, what is obligatory and what is permissible or forbidden, what is desirable and what is undesirable, what is urgent and what can wait, and so forth.

Thus the structures in which a society is organized constitute a focus of inclusions and exclusions, possibilities and difficulties, openings and closings, resistances and frailties, which limit and orientate any activity developing within those social structures. But it is within social structures that any religion—in each concrete case—has to function, and these social structures do not permit just any activity to develop within them, but only certain activities. And even these activities are limited and channeled to some extent by these same social structures.

The structure of each society, then, *limits* and *orientates* the possibilities for action and any religion within it. Consequently, when we say that no religion functions in a vacuum, but is always a socially situated reality, what we mean is that any religion's activity is *limited* and *orientated* by its social context.

Chapter Eight

RELIGION AND SOCIAL MODE OF PRODUCTION

We are going to adopt, with a provisory and partial character, the sociological hypothesis that the central structure of every society, its *infrastructure*,[44] is constituted by a population's specific organization in relation to its material (its natural and developed) resources, in view of the satisfaction of its needs. This system of organization of a population in relation to its material resources for the production of goods destined for the (direct or indirect) satisfaction of its needs is often called its *mode of production*.[45]

It is our position that it is a society's mode of production that constitutes its central structure, its infrastructure. We take this position because it seems quite clear that the social activity of the production of goods necessary for the survival of the members of a society (and for the perpetuation of each society as a living human group, generation after generation) is indeed the basic and fundamental activity of every society.

Perhaps it is the *only* constant and indispensable activity in any society. Why? First, because the material activity performed in order to produce and reproduce human life is an ongoing and indispensable activity in any society. If this activity ceased, human beings would perish. Secondly, because each and all of the members of any society are (directly or indirectly) linked to this activity, continuously. This activity produces everything they use, from food to communications media. When individuals totally detach themselves from this activity system, they perish. Thirdly, because, in consequence, this activity is a *conditio sine qua non* for every other activity, individual or collective. It is the activity that makes possible and supports all other human activities, including, for our purposes, religious beliefs and practices.

In order to stay alive, then, every human population must organize itself in relation to the material resources available, in order to produce the indispensable means of its survival. The organization of this activity of production and reproduction of human life (and of the adequate means for maintaining this human life) is called a society's *mode of production*. This mode of production, which varies among populations according to the material

44

resources available, constitutes the central structure, the *infrastructure*, of any society. We make this assertion, as we have seen, in view of the fact that the specific activity of the production and reproduction of human life (and of the adequate means for it) is an activity that is (1) constant, (2) indispensable to every society, (3) common to all living human beings, together and severally, directly or indirectly, and (4) a necessary condition for the possibility and ongoing support of any other human activity, individual or collective.

Every human population, therefore, organizes itself in relation to its available material resources, in order to produce and reproduce the life of this population in some particular space. The specific manner in which this population organizes to this end constitutes its particular mode of production. This mode of production involves a structured set of social relations. It regulates the access of the various individuals and groups composing the society to the different *means of production* (that is, to all the different instruments—machines, roads, land, seed, and so on—that can serve to produce goods capable of satisfying the various human needs). It regulates the distribution of the population's productive capabilities—that is, the organization of the community *work force* (who is going to produce what, and how, and where). Finally, it regulates the distribution of the *finished product*, now ready for consumption (who is going to dispose of which goods, and how, when, and where).[46]

There is not just one, but *many* modes of production in the world today, and in the history of humanity. The specific mode of production regulating the life of a determined society in a particular historical era does not depend only, or even mainly, on mere chance or on the free will of its members. No, in the very first place it depends on the concrete conditions of a given population—the number of its members, the natural resources it has available, the instruments of work ready to hand, acquired experience and knowledge, the usages and customs of this particular people, and so forth.

This whole set of given concrete conditions of a group is what will decide which modes of production are possible for it, and which are impossible. There will always be *several* possible modes of production (and an indefinite number that are imaginable but concretely impossible). But among the various modes of production possible in a concrete situation, each population, at least in the course of a given stage of its development, will organize itself in one only.

Each human population, then, has its own mode of production. And as we have said, each society's specific mode of production constitutes the central structure, the infrastructure, of that concrete society. In regulating access to the means of production, distribution of the work force, and apportionment of products, this mode of production will also regulate, although only indirectly, other important aspects of social life. It will define, indirectly, which activities (other than production) will be *impossible*; which will be possible but *undesirable*; which possible activities will be merely *tolerated*, and just how far; which will be *acceptable*, but only on a secondary level; which, besides being possible and acceptable, will be advantageous; and finally, among the last-named, which will be *primary* or *urgent*.

When we said that a religion is *situated*, always, in a specific social context, we were preparing to posit the following hypothesis: *every religion is situated in a specific mode of production*. Likewise, when we stressed that every religion is limited and orientated by its social context, we were already stating, in a general way, this first hypothetical conclusion: *the activity of any religion is limited and orientated by the specific mode of production within which it functions*.

To put this in still another way, the form in which a population organizes itself with regard to the material resources available to it, in order to produce goods destined for the maintenance and reproduction of its life—the form of social organization of that society's production—conditions, we repeat, the activity of any religion that may arise within it. That is, the form of social organization of production conditions which religious activities are impossible, which are possible but undesirable, which are tolerable and how far, which are acceptable but only secondarily, which religious activities—if any—are advantageous, and, finally, which—if any—are primary and urgent (independently, again, of the consciousness or intentions of the religion's representatives).

A society's specific mode of production fixes the *limits* within which any religion can function in that society, and likewise outlines the *tendencies* within which such a religion will function there. Thus the specific mode of production of each particular society will condition the most likely possibilities and impossibilities, the importance, the meaning, the functions, the organizational forms, the discourse, the practices, the development, the transformations, and the dispersion, or propagation, that each religion can hope to attain, and actually does attain, within this particular society.[47]

Chapter Nine

RELIGION IN
CLASS SOCIETIES

We have emphasized above that the central structure, the infrastructure, of every society—the social structure that supplies the concrete *basis*, fixes the *limits*, and traces the fundamental *orientations* of the structuration and development of any other social activity (including, for our purposes, any religion)—is a structure constituted by what we are calling the *mode of production* of that society. And we have made it clear that by "mode of production" we understand the form in which a population organizes itself, in relation to the material resources available to it, in order to produce the goods that will permit this human population to maintain itself in life and to perpetuate itself.

As we have already emphasized briefly, this form, manner, or mode of organizing social production depends first and foremost on the *content* it can manage to organize in and by that productivity. That is, it depends on the available *population* (twenty human beings cannot produce according to the same form as twenty thousand). It depends on the *natural resources* available to that population (production is not the same in the Sahara as in the San Fernando Valley). It depends on the set of *instruments of labor* in the hands of that population (it is very different to farm with instruments of stone instead of with oxen and iron plows). It depends on the *experience and knowledge acquired* by this population (a herd of oxen serves for nothing if its uses are not known and understood), and the *usages and customs* of this population (a herd of swine is of no use if swine are considered either sacred or harmful).[48]

Such, then, is the content upon which the form, or mode, of production depends. But this organizable content renders *several* modes of production possible, not just one.[49] What, then, will determine that it will be mode of production *x*, rather than *y* or *z*, among the various feasible modes, that a population will adopt? It seems to me that this will *not* depend on the content organizable for production. That content determines which modes of production are *possible*, not which will be actual.

The actual mode of production will depend on other factors. It will depend

47

on (1) the *traditional mode of production* of a given population, (2) the *internal social relationships* that have developed within a given mode of production when it appears necessary to organize a different mode, and (3) the *external social relationships* that bind this population, at this time, with other human groups.

Communitarian vs. Asymmetric Modes of Production

The various modes of production can all be classified under two general categories.[50] There are *communitarian* modes, in which all members of a society enjoy equal access to the existing means of production (so that private appropriation of these means is excluded). They entail an egalitarian distribution of the labor force, with a fairly equal amount of productive work required of each of the members of the community—without privileges or other exceptions beyond those deriving from one's physical capacity for work, and with a division of labor that is fairly simple and flexible. And they entail an egalitarian distribution of the finished products of the work (varying only according to needs due to the age or health of the individuals).

Then there are *asymmetric* modes of production, in which only a permanent minority controls the principal means of production (that is, the means are its private property). The work force of the population is systematically distributed in an unequal manner (and includes those who exercise no directly productive function—namely, those who have control of the most important means of production). The finished products of the labor are systematically distributed in a proportionately unequal manner (assigning a larger portion to the controllers of this distribution—that is, to these same private proprietors of the means of production).[51]

In the present study we shall be referring much more to asymmetric modes of production, and their sociological implications for religion, than to communitarian modes.[52]

Let us begin by noting that when a society organizes in an asymmetric mode of production, whatever be the reasons for this organization, it generates a progressive process of *structuration of the society into social classes*, with notably differing degrees of power, with relationships of dominance, and objectively opposing interests.[53]

A society organized in an asymmetric mode of production will tend to restructure its population by dividing it. That is, a certain minority will gradually increase its power. It has in its control (1) the means of production necessary for the survival of the members of the society, all and severally. It controls (2) the distribution of the work force of the whole population of the society, to the point where this minority can abandon its own direct participation in production and force the majority to produce according to the criteria of the minority. And it controls (3) the distribution of the goods indispensable for the survival of the members of the society, all and severally, to the point where this minority can amass for its own consumption (or exchange) a greater quantity of goods than remains in the hands of the majority.

Correlatively, the process of establishment of an asymmetric mode of production will tend to place the majority in a situation of subordination. It will see itself dispossessed, little by little, of (1) control over the use and distribution of the means of production, (2) control over the distribution of the work force, so that the majority is forced to labor under the control of others in order to obtain the goods necessary for survival, and (3) control over the distribution of the goods necessary for survival, even to the point of inability to survive—for instance, in cases of scarcity.

In such a type of production—the one that predominates in Latin America, be it remembered—unequal power over production (distribution and application of means of production, distribution of the work force and of goods produced) will entail *relationships of dominance* among the groups that will be splitting off from one another by reason of that very production.

A minority will come to constitute a group of *dominant classes* (as they gradually acquire power over access to the means of production, the distribution of the labor force and of goods produced), and will be able to augment their authority over the work, repose, life, and health of their fellows. The majority of the members of such a society will come to constitute a group of *dominated classes*, as they are gradually dispossessed of their power over means of production, distribution of their own labor force, and division of the goods they themselves produce and need. They will see their participation in decisions concerning their own labor, repose, health, and life gradually reduced.

The fate of the majority will be ever more and more controlled not by itself but by a minority. The minority will decide the working conditions of the majority without sharing those conditions, a minority that does not participate in the production of goods but appropriates them and decides on their distribution.

This is what we mean when we speak of "dominance," or "social relationships of dominance," or a mode of production that structures society into "dominators and dominated." We mean that a minority decides the fate of the majority because it possesses the means to decide it. For it possesses the social means of production of the goods necessary for the survival of the population.

In this type of societal organization, relationships of dominance (arising from power over production) lead to a position of *opposing interests* between the two major segments of the population. The members of the dominant minority, proprietors of the principal means of production, are objectively interested in maintaining an asymmetric organization of production and continuing to dominate and to increase their power. The others, the dominated majority, those whose principal means of production have been expropriated, are objectively interested in not continuing to be dominated, in reducing the power of the dominators, and in restructuring the prevailing mode of production.

This opposition of interests does not depend so much upon the intentions or awareness of the individuals and groups involved, as upon the real, objective situation obtaining within the process of production. Individuals and groups that by war, inheritance, luck, social climbing, and the like, have acquired great power over the organization of production, spontaneously and unconsciously strive to preserve, and if possible augment, their power, and prevent access to it by the majority.[54] On the other hand the groups whose power over the organization of production has been expropriated tend for their part, with equal spontaneity and unconsciousness, to try to transform the relationships of power with respect to production (in detriment of the power of the minority). Hence we speak of *objectively* opposing interests—for these interests do not depend on the will or awareness of the individuals, but on the objective situation obtaining in the social organization of productive activity.

Religion in a Society Conditioned by Asymmetric Production

No religion situated in a class society functions only within a "society," or within a "mode of production." These are abstractions, however useful and objectively verifiable they may be. No, any religion operates first and foremost *in the midst of concrete social classes*, with their different degrees of power, their mutual relationships arising from dominance, and their objectively opposing interests. The central, the fundamental, structure of a society with an asymmetric mode of production is an *objectively conflictive structure of social dominance.* Such a structure of class societies cuts across, limits, and orientates all the activities performed by the individuals and groups that make it up—independently of the conscious intentions of these individuals and groups.

Thus the religious activity of any group of believers within a class society is an activity objectively *situated* within an objectively conflictive structure of social dominance. This objective situation—the situation of any religion in a class society, and therefore a situation independent of the awareness or will of the representatives of a religion—will *cut across, limit,* and *orientate* the activity of the religious institutions (and of the faithful who make them up) within this society.

In other words, an objectively conflictive structure of social dominance—which is the presiding structure in class societies—will condition in a particular manner which religious activities are impossible within it, which are possible but undesirable, which are tolerable and to what point, which are acceptable but only secondarily, which are suitable, and which are primary or urgent. And it will do this independently of the awareness and will of those who perform the religious activities.

The conflictive structure of dominance of any class society establishes—in a specific manner linked to the differentiation of *classes* within it and the asymmetric relationships of *power* among these classes—the *limits* within which any religion can function in it, and the *tendencies* that will permeate and orientate the activity of this religion in this society. Thus this class structure will condition the possibilities and the impossibilities, the importance, the meaning, the thought patterns, the practices, the organization, the development, the propagation, and the probable transformations that any religion can objectively expect (and actually achieve) within such a society.

To sum up very briefly what we have sought to express up to this point in Part II, let us put the same thing in another way. It is not simply, and not even mainly, the "goodwill" or "good fortune" of a group of believers, or religious leaders, that will define the development and the end product of their religious activity. No, it is mainly—more than anything else—the structure of the society in which they act that will define what forms of activity it is more feasible for them to develop (and which, however bravely they may be sought, are simply impossible). It will also determine what the more probable results of such activity will be (even when these results are energetically repudiated by the religious exponents, who may have earnestly tried to avoid them).

Next, in view of all that has been said, we shall direct our attention to a few of the types of social organization that are pertinent for a sociological analysis of religions in Latin America. We shall endeavor to identify some of the central conflicts within them, as well as the limits and tendencies that such conflicts impose on religious activity.

Chapter Ten

RELIGION IN
PRE-COLUMBIAN SOCIETIES

To begin, I am not going to suggest that pre-Columbian Latin American societies exhibited only one type of social organization, or only one mode of production.[55] We shall be examining only the *type* of the social organization of those societies—that is, the set of traits that are found to be common to those really very different communities (and their modes of production), especially as pertaining to a sociology of religions in contemporary Latin America.

Everything the current state of research has been able to determine seems to indicate that the indigenous Latin American communities each had *a single religious system*. It must be pointed out, however, that religion in those communities does not present itself as a differentiated institution, separate from the other dimensions of collective life—economic dimensions, for instance, or political, or military, or family. On the contrary, religion appears inextricably bound up with these other dimensions.

We can state it in this way: in those communities there was a *minimal degree (or no degree at all) of social differentiation of religious activity.*[56] That is, all the activities that we would spontaneously tend to perceive distinctly as "religious" had a bearing that was directly economic, political, educational, and so forth. And conversely, those communities lived all other dimensions of their collective life in constant reference to the religious dimension—that is, to those supernatural and metasocial forces in which they believed, on which they felt dependent, and before which they felt themselves bound to a certain code of conduct. This reference is, it would appear from the research, central.

This *fundamentally religious perception of the world* (closely bound up with the single, almost undifferentiated, religious system of each of those communities) seems to be one of the factors that made such communities so resistant to and mistrustful of any teaching or practice that was antireligious, or even nonreligious.

To boot, the properly religious practices of those native communities (and this is one of the factors that renders religion all but indistinguishable from their other activities) exhibit a minimal degree (or none at all) of bureaucratization, or hierarchical organization of specialists in the religious sphere. In those communities there were but few individuals dedicated exclusively to a specifically religious activity. And those few individuals were differentiated in a way that was relatively simple, and inextricably bound up, once more, with the "other" activities of the community—economic, political, hygienic activities, and so on.

Finally, the distinctly religious teaching produced, propagated, and shared within those communities is a teaching developed to a *minimal degree of complexity and systematization*. Religious teaching significantly different from other discourse is relatively limited (limited to what would be accessible to the conscious memory of the individual). The separate and discrete elements of its structure are minimal in number and expressed in relatively simple relationships.[57]

To sum up: the native Latin American communities are characterized, from the viewpoint of the sociologist of religions, by (1) a basically religious perception of the world, (2) a single religious system in each community, (3) a minimal degree of social differentiation of religious activity, (4) a minimal degree of bureaucratization of religious practices, and (5) a minimal degree of complexity and systematization of religious doctrine.

And yet between the Aztecs, Mayas, Incas, and Chibchas on the one hand, and the Caribs, Guaranís, and Waraos on the other, there were certainly notable differences in their religious systems, especially in respect to the third, fourth, and fifth characteristics listed just above. We can stress the common elements between the two groups, of course—but why the differences? Why was there a notably greater degree of social differentiation of religious activity, bureaucratization of religious practices, and systemization of religious thought among the Aztecs, Mayas, Incas, and Chibchas than among the Caribs, Guaranís, and Waraos?

Everything seems to indicate that these differences arose precisely out of the difference in the modes of production between these two groupings of indigenous communities—and especially out of a difference on the following levels of the mode of production: (1) the number of individuals in the community, (2) the number of different means of production, and (3) the number of differentiated productive occupations and specialized groups in the community (division of labor).

Indeed, each of these levels is more highly developed, quantitatively speaking, in the first group of native cultures mentioned (the Aztecs, Mayas, Incas, and Chibchas) than in the second (the Caribs, Guaranís, and Waraos).

Pierre Bourdieu has proposed a hypothesis here: in the presence of a greater *social division of collective labor*, the possibilities and needs increase for a greater *division of religious functions*.[58] This hypothesis seems adequate to explain the differences we have noted between the two groupings of pre-Columbian communities with regard to their respective religions.

Let me explain what I mean. The greater the number of members of a community, the greater are its needs. Now, if to the greater number of members we add a relative scarcity of natural resources available for the satisfaction of these needs, the necessity for productive work on the part of each of the individuals of the community will be that much greater. Likewise greater will be the demand for relatively stable groups within the community to concentrate on and specialize in different, complementary activities, to assure the satisfaction of all the needs of the population. In such conditions, the development of a social division of labor is practically inescapable.[59] That is, the appearance and institutionalization of distinct occupations, each performed by a stable group within the community, is almost bound to occur.

When (for these and other reasons) the institutionalization of a social division of collective labor is introduced into a community, it becomes much more likely that all its important activities, religion included, will begin to be socially differentiated. The social differentiation of a collective activity has as a result, generally speaking, that one group within the community specializes in precisely this differentiation, and that the community eventually reproduces within itself the collective tendency toward a progressive division of labor. That is, there is a tendency for the community to *bureaucratize*.

An activity such as religious activity, in which linguistic expression, oral or written—that is, discursive production—is basic, will have a tendency, in proportion as it differentiates itself socially, specializes, and bureaucratizes, to have its self-expression reflect the social conditions of production—which are conditions proper to a progressive division of labor.

Religious activity will, then, tend increasingly to be an activity that *complexifies and systematizes itself*. The differentiated and hierarchized groups resulting from a progressive division of religious functions will be reflected in the complexity of its linguistic self-expression.

Nevertheless, rather than these differentiating traits, what we wish to emphasize in the religion of the pre-Columbian communities are their *common* traits. For the differences are small in comparison with post-Columbian Latin American communities.

Chapter Eleven

RELIGION IN
THE COLONIAL ERA

In the sixteenth century, a reorganization of the indigenous societies, with the exploitation of the natural resources of their ecosystem, was undertaken in Latin America. This colonial enterprise, principally begun and imposed by Spain and Portugal and developed in view of their economic needs, involved the radical transformation of all aspects of the life of the indigenous communities, including their religions.

European Background

In order to understand the importance of the religious aspect in the Luso-Hispanic colonization of America, it will be useful to have a sketch of the situation of religion in a feudal regime, the mode of production governing social organization in Spain and Portugal at that time.

The type of regime that preceded the establishment of the national states in Europe, throughout the so-called Middle Ages (especially from the eighth century onward), was that of feudalism. Under feudalism, the peasant communities scattered throughout Europe were subjected to the dominion of feudal lords. They were their vassals (*feudales*, chattels). In these conditions the peasantry was forced to either produce more goods than were necessary for its own survival, or else retrench from those necessities, in order to meet the demands of the feudal lords—in the form of first-fruits, tithes, and other tributes. Furthermore, the peasants, in their capacity as vassals or servants of the feudal lords, were not only forced into economic subordination, but underwent as well a subjection—lifelong—of their very persons to the owners of the fields they worked. The men were obliged to serve them as soldiers in their wars, the young women as their companions of the night. Both men and women, and their children, could be sold, along with the lands, to other masters.

The peasant communities derived no economic benefit whatever from the feudal relationship. Quite the contrary. Hence on the part of the peasants there was no economic motivation to perpetuate a feudal nexus with the lords. The lords, on the other hand, did derive economic benefit from the feudal relationship. They therefore had an objective need to perpetuate the feudal nexus. That is, they had an objective need to maintain the peasant communities in a condition of subjection and servitude.

How could a social relationship, in whose maintenance and perpetuation only one of its member groups had an objective interest, be perpetuated? There would seem to be only two ways to insure the continuation of the feudal relationship between lords and servants: imposition by force of arms, and persuasion by force of religion.

And indeed the history of the subjection of the European peasantry under feudal sway was marked by the intimate collaboration of armed violence and religious persuasion—the "alliance of throne and altar." Inasmuch as feudal Europe—like pre-Columbian Latin America—had a preeminently religious vision of the world, the forging of a religious link between peasants and lords became a matter of necessity for the dominant aristocracy (independently of its awareness and its intentions.)[60] Thus the feudal aristocracy found itself obliged (we might almost say, *spontaneously*) to have recourse to the Catholic clergy, with whom it had close economic, religious, and family bonds, to legitimate the feudal regimen—for its own conscience' sake no less than for that of the peasantry.

The limitations and tendencies inherent in the conflictive structure of domination in the feudal mode of production, then, gradually led to a restructuration of the European religious presence. In this restructuration, traditional religious beliefs of vastly different European peasant communities were all subjected to a *monopolistic religious system*, that of the Catholic Church.[61] This monopoly did not mean, strictly speaking, the establishment of a single religion common to the whole of Europe—but neither did it mean the coexistence of various religious systems on the same level. Rather it meant the presence of one *predominant* religious system, with power sufficient to eliminate, assimilate, subordinate, or marginalize preexistent ones.

This religious system occupied a central place in the feudal regimen, owing to two traits of that regimen: independently of the consciousness or will of religious representatives, (1) the peasants' worldview was preponderantly religious, and (2) the feudal lords had an objective need for recourse to an extraeconomic nexus in order to perpetuate their economic relationship with the tillers of the soil.

These two traits of the feudal regimen led the Catholic clergy (independently of its consciousness and will, here as well), to establish itself as the *central institution for the perpetuation of feudal society.*[62] That is, the clergy came to be restructured with a view to the consolidation of feudalism. The clergy also took up a monopolistic position central to the process of perpetuating the domination of lords over servants.

In a society that was *heterogeneous* (built upon forced unification of diverse and traditionally autonomous societies), *conflictive* (characterized by relationships of dominance among groups with objectively opposing interests), and with a marked *social division of labor*, as was European feudal society, a social institution such as the Catholic Church was constrained to implement a notable *social differentiation of religious activity*. This constraint was all the stronger owing to the effort required of the church to effect this differentiation in conflict with the diverse traditional religious systems of European peasant communities.

However, the social differentiation of religious activity did not exclude the Catholic clergy from the exercise of economic, political, juridical, and military functions. On the contrary, it was precisely the multifunctionality of the clergy that obliged it to take up and maintain its central position in the consolidation of the feudal system.

The social differentiation of the religious activity of the church involved, as a parallel, specialization by stable groups as professional functionaries of religious activities, especially in the urban centers. These functionaries gradually organized themselves into a very complex hierarchy. This hierarchy—numerous, heterogeneous, and subject to the limitations and orientations of feudal structure—occasioned a *high degree of bureaucratization of religious practices*. The bureaucracy was structured in the image and likeness of the feudal structure itself. The result was that the religious self-expression produced by this ecclesiastical hierarchy—a self-expression limited and orientated by the conditions peculiar to the feudal regime—became *notably diversified, complex, and systematized*—just as were the bureaucracy that produced it, and the society wherein that bureaucracy functioned.

European Implantation

The Conquistadores arriving in Latin America from the sixteenth century onward had come from just this context. Sons of the feudally organized societies of Spain and Portugal, financed and directed by the dominant groups of those same societies, they were, both objectively and subjectively, bearers of feudal structures.

After eight centuries of close ties with feudalism, the activity of the Catholic Church in Latin America was of course limited and orientated by the same factors that had structured it within the European society of that time. At once pressured and bolstered by the military superiority of the European armies over those of the indigenous populations of the New World, the Catholic Church of course undertook religious activities showing the same traits that had marked its European history. The church erected itself into a monopolistic religious system by eliminating, assimilating, subordinating, or marginalizing the indigenous religious systems. It took its position as a multifunctional institution with a central role in the perpetuation of society. It reproduced itself as a socially differentiated, bureaucratized organization elaborating a multiple, complex, and systematized self-expression.

Pre-Hispanic Latin America being what it was, the enterprise undertaken by the church enjoyed great possibilities of success. To a certain extent, it fulfilled them.

Chapter Twelve

RELIGION IN THE DEPENDENT CAPITALIST SYSTEM

During the nineteenth century, Latin America underwent a series of victorious wars of independence against Spanish colonial hegemony. Europe, meanwhile, was suffering the death throes of feudalism as the capitalist system replaced it industrially, commercially, politically, and culturally.

Capitalism in Europe

Capitalism, which was already becoming the dominant system on a world scale, was forcing a radical reorganization of European life. Capitalism had arisen in the eighteenth century, bringing Europe from a decentralized agricultural economy based on small-scale production by peasants, to an industrial economy concentrated on urban manufacture. It had moved Europe from a family economy to a mass economy, from a relatively autarkic subsistence economy to an interdependent economy of overproduction for international trade, from an economy based on direct consumption by the producer (further narrowed by the exigencies of tribute to be paid to feudal lords) to an economy based on monetary payment and workers' salaries. It had moved Europe from an economy subject to the cycles of nature to an economy subject to an identical schedule the year round. And, finally, capitalism had brought Europe from an economy in which laborers owned the instruments with which they worked the soil, and worked it in accordance with natural conditions, their own needs, and the obligations of tribute, to an economy in which laborers possessed only their own labor—and provided it in accordance with the exigencies of industry.

The whole of European society felt the influence of the capitalistic reorganization of the economy—down to the smallest of life's details. Forced to migrate en masse to the cities, where the factories were, the peasants saw their customs changing and their traditional bonds dissolving. With their migration, the feudal lords, and eventually the whole nobility, gradually lost their power and wealth. An accelerating division and subdivision of labor reached into every corner of European civilization.

Soon, in order to live, one had to purchase consumer goods in the flourishing marketplace. But in order to purchase those goods, money was needed; and in order to have money, one had to own a factory, a bank, or a business— or else (more usually) one had to have a paid job in industry or a bank or business. Economic activity, ever more and more differentiated from all other human activities, was now gradually converted into the central activity of European society. And those who controlled it—the burghers, the new middle class on the increase, formed by the industrialists, bankers, and businessmen of the burgs, or larger towns—were coming little by little to form the dominant class of the new society.

Meanwhile the laboring class, ever growing in numbers from the migration of the peasant population, was beginning to form the most important dominated class of Europe. Among the reasons for the importance of this new laboring class were its dizzying increase in numbers, the density of its concentrations, its misery, its combativeness, and the ever more indispensable contribution of its labor to the production and reproduction of the necessary means of subsistence for the inhabitants of Europe.

Capitalism and the Christian Churches

The progressive consolidation of capitalism as the dominant mode of production had a violent impact on the situation of religion in Europe. The Christian churches (plural now, ever since the Protestant Reformation in the sixteenth century) saw a strange, indifferent, sometimes hostile, world rise up around them. They began to undergo a profound crisis at the hands of the emergent capitalism.[63]

Among the causes of the crisis of religion in general and of the Christian churches in particular was the new character of social relationships under capitalism. As economic activity became a differentiated activity and the central activity in capitalistic society, it created distinct classes, in every European society. In particular, it created the basic classes of the capitalist mode of production—the bourgeoisie and the proletariat.

These two classes were intimately connected to one another by a bond that was basically economic. In capitalism, manual laborers (like nearly every other group of persons whose means of production had been expropriated), were forced to sell their labor in exchange for a salary to live on. That is, for exclusively economic reasons, workers were obliged, objectively (independently of their awareness and intentions), to go to those who owned the means of production and offer their labor in exchange for a salary that would enable them to survive. But in parallel fashion the owners of the means of production, in order to set these means in motion, were objectively forced, for purely economic reasons, to go to the individuals who had been dispossessed of these means of production and purchase their labor in exchange for a salary sufficient for the daily maintenance and continuation, without major problems, of this same labor.

Thus this basic relationship of production, constitutive of the capitalist system, tended to reproduce itself for purely economic motives. In this type of society, religion was no longer indissolubly linked to the rest of human activity, as it was in pre-Columbian Latin American communities. Nor did it any longer occupy the central position in economic relationships, as it had in feudal societies. And all this was not for reasons deriving from the consciousness or will of religious agents. These were limitations and tendencies deriving from the very structure of capitalist society. They imposed themselves on all the activities that the members of such a society developed, including the theorization and praxis of religion.

Thus, in the transition from feudalism to capitalism, the Catholic Church ceased to exercise a religious monopoly. Catholicism was obliged to form part of a *divided religious field*, with relationships of competition (and, in certain cases, of domination) among the various religious systems present.

This divided religious sphere tends to lose its central role in the perpetuation of social relationships, yielding this position to a set of institutions more directly connected with economic activity. As a consequence, in capitalism, religions tends to exercise a *subsidiary role* in the reproduction of social relationships.

In conjunction with these two processes, the increasing social division of labor entails a *definitive social differentiation of religious institutions.* That is, the division of labor comes to involve a clear delimitation of properly religious activities, and a marked tendency to separate them, institutionally, from other human activities—economic, political, juridical, military, scientific, and so on.

At the same time, the various religious institutions present within the framework of capitalism undergo a process of division and subdivision of labor. This leads them to a *much more marked bureaucratization* of their own organization, as they gradually lose the monarchical coloring that characterized them under feudalism and replace it with certain traits more typical of a liberal-bourgeois parliamentary democracy, such as consultation, elections, collegial decision-making, institutionalization of conflicts.

Finally, religious self-expression manifests significant transformations in its own structure. It develops, in capitalism, an *extreme diversification, complexification, and systematization*—even assimilating a multiplicity of *contradictory self-expressions,* which of course further increases the complexity of discursive production in the area of religion.

Capitalism in Latin America

Capitalism began to penetrate Latin America toward the end of the nineteenth century and the beginning of the twentieth. Bolstered by its predominance in Europe, little by little it became the dominant mode of production on our continent as well.

Therewith and thereby it inaugurated a new process of reorganization of

Latin American societies. This restructuration of society, orientated by the capitalistic mode of production, involved important implications for the religions of our continent. Latin America now embarked on a course of (1) establishment of a divided religious area, with one church predominant, (2) reduction of the religious area, objectively as well as subjectively, to a secondary place in Latin American society, (3) the separation of the religious area, with an increasing degree of differentiation, from other social institutions, (4) a process of bureaucratization more and more open to consultation, pressure, and conflict, and (5) a rather more complex, systematized, and conflictive religious self-expression than this continent had heretofore known.

At any rate, this is one way to interpret the more recent history of religion in Latin America.

Chapter Thirteen

RELIGION IN A COMPLEX SOCIETY

Society, in every Latin American nation, is a complex society. It seems to me of the first importance to emphasize this in an essay on the relationships between the religious area and social conflicts in Latin America. And it would probably be equally important for the vast majority of the nations of our planet today.

When we call Latin American society "complex," we mean that the basic structure of Latin American societies is organized not in a single, isolated mode of production—in no Latin American country would this be verified— but in an *articulated set of several coexistent modes of production.*[64]

The history of Latin America since the sixteenth century has consisted in the partially successful attempt to restructure the different traditional forms of production *on the initiative of, under the patronage of,* and *in service to* modes of production proper to other societies. At the same time, this history of Latin America has also been the history of an attempt, likewise partially successful, to unify the multiple, extremely divergent, and, from ancient times, autonomous, pre-Columbian modes of production. This attempt arose first on the part of the great European colonial powers. It was then renewed by the great capitalist powers, especially the United States. This process has continued even to our own day.

This process has resulted in a situation peculiar to contemporary Latin America. In Latin America we find societies in which various modes of production coexisted in their differences until they were subjected to a process of restructuration under a single mode of production, the semifeudal mode imposed during the Luso-Hispanic colonial period. Now, once more today, these modes of production are being reorganized, this time under another dominant mode of production, the capitalist mode. But this capitalism, in its own turn, is, like its semifeudal predecessor, dependent upon the organization of production in non-Latin American societies. This resulted, in the first instance, from the necessity of importing from the industrialized countries the technology needed for the capitalistic development of Latin America.

In the particular perspective that we have assumed for our investigation of religion in Latin America, this situation presents two aspects of interest to sociology.

1. A Divided Religious Field

Pre-Columbian societies each had one (and one only) particular religion, situated, in each concrete case, within a single mode of production. It exerted upon that religion the limitations and orientations proper to this or that particular mode of production.

In the post-Columbian process, these indigenous societies, together with their respective religious systems, were placed in a forced relationship among themselves, under the domination of a new mode of production—one which, as we have seen, was closely linked to the Catholic Church. This complicated enormously the social focus of the delimitations and orientations that, in Latin America, conditioned the religious field of each of those societies. At the same time, the religious field itself became diversified and complexified, organized as it was under the monopoly of a religion originally linked to a foreign society.

Hence, with some few exceptions, we can no longer speak of a single religion, limited and orientated by the structure of a single mode of production. Instead, now we have to refer to a divided religious field, situated in a focus of (contradictory and asymmetric) limitations and orientations generated by a *macrostructure of asymmetrically articulated modes of production*—that is, under one dominant mode of production.

2. A Religious Field in Conflict

The pre-Columbian societies of our continent that were organized in an asymmetric mode of production—the Incas, Aztecs, Chibchas, Mayas, and others—each had a single specific class structure. This class structure constituted a social focus of conflictive limitations and orientations, which exerted their influence upon the single particular religion of each of those societies. Once colonization began, the asymmetric societies (like the symmetric ones, the Guaranís, for instance) were now subjected to a restructuring, directed toward a new class division corresponding to the current dominant mode of production (first the colonial semifeudal mode, then the dependent semicapitalist mode).

Now the population of Latin America began to undergo a process in which individuals and groups were repositioned in new social classes. Even in cases where their traditional structures were partially preserved, a new social relationship was imposed from without in the form of a relationship of subordination. In the midst of such restructuring, it is no longer possible, except in special cases, to speak of a religion situated in a single class structure. Rather it becomes necessary to speak of a religious field positioned in a *conflictive process of restructuration of the class division* of a given society.

This process (1) is generated by the macrostructure of asymmetrically articulated modes of production under a dominant mode of production, and (2) determines the specific traits of the social focus of the (contradictory and asymmetric) limitations and orientations brought to bear on the religious area by this macrostructure.

To say all this in another way, and thereby conclude this chapter: the objectively conflictive structure of social domination of a complex society (such as that of Latin America) fixes in a special way the *limits* within which a religion can operate within that society. It also traces, proportionately to these limits, the different *tendencies* that permeate and orientate any activity that a religion may deploy there.

This structure will condition, in its own way, the possibilities and impossibilities, the importance and the meaning, the externalized self-understanding and the practices, the propagation and the transformations, that any religion can objectively hope to achieve (and will actually achieve) in such a society—always independently of the awareness and intentions of the exponents of religion.

Chapter Fourteen

RELIGION AND CLASS CONFLICTS

We have made it clear that every religion is situated within a specific social context—or more exactly, within a specific mode of production. We have explained how such a context established a focus of limitations and orientations that condition the activity of any religion within it. Then we referred to the peculiarities of class societies, and the specific manner in which class structure conditions the activity of any religion within it. Next we rapidly examined the three historical types of situations in which Latin American religions successively found themselves. Last of all we sought to delineate in general terms the complex structures of our societies today, and the implications of this complexity for the religions, especially the Catholic Church, that function within them today.

But in all this we have dealt only in generalities. We have not delved into the specific relationships of the religious sphere in Latin America with the different social classes in conflict in our societies today. This is what we shall now attempt to do. We do not pretend to exhaust the subject, but we shall attempt to sketch certain hypotheses, and certain problems, which will be able to serve as an orientation to researchers as they come to grips with this thorny set of problems.

Latin American societies are "class societies." What does this mean? It means that here in Latin America the production of the goods necessary to keep human beings alive, as well as the acquisition of such goods, is organized in an unequal or asymmetric manner.

Organization is asymmetric as to (1) *access to the means of production.* Only certain groups have control of the large-scale means of production (the larger banks, plantations, industries). Others have control of the medium-sized means of production (middle-sized farms and factories, for instance). Still others control only small-scale means of production (for example, workshops). Finally, there are those who lack all control over means of production (rural and urban employees and laborers).

Organization of the production of goods necessary to keep human beings alive is likewise asymmetric as to (2) the *distribution of the labor force.* There are those who have great power over the distribution of the work force,

throughout vast sectors of the population (especially large landowners, industrialists, and business executives). There are those who have some power
over at least the distribution of their own labor (small landowners, for instance, as well as certain professional persons, technicians, and business persons). Finally there are those who can survive only by selling their labor to the
highest bidder (farmhands, day laborers, some technicians and other employees belonging to the proletariat, and so on).

Organization of goods necessary to keep human beings alive is also asymmetric as to (3) the *division of the end product* of human labor. There are
those who have a practically unlimited power over this division (major industrialists, bankers, business executives, plantation owners). There are those
who have comfortable access to the products necessary to support their
families (middle-income landowners, professionals, middle- and high-
management persons, and so on). And there are those who have the barest
capability, if any at all, of acquiring the necessary minimum for their daily
survival (agricultural and industrial laborers, schoolteachers, employees paid
hourly wages, peddlers, and the like).

Division of Labor, Division of Power

Such a division of labor (more accentuated in capitalism) entails a marked
inequality in the principal dimensions of human life in society—nutrition,
clothing, lodging, hygiene, education, repose, recreation, and so on. But inequality in these areas of concrete human life is at bottom only the effect of
an unequal *power* over the production and distribution of the goods indispensable for the satisfaction of human needs. Whereas a tiny minority is in
possession of enormous capital, enabling it to control the major means of
production, the vast majority lacks all capital, hence all control over means
of production. Whereas a minority retains enormous power to make decisions concerning its own existence and that of the other members of society,
the majority has a minimal power of decision even where its own subsistence
is concerned.

Hence it should come as no surprise that this situation gives rise to a conflict of interests.[65] It cuts across all dimensions of social life, and touches
every individual and group within such a society—independently of their
awareness or intentions in this respect. It is a matter of conflict between
classes objectively interested in preserving and reaping the benefits of a social
structure in which they occupy a dominant position, and classes interested in
one way or another in transforming this same structure, in which they occupy
a subordinate position.

Religion within Class Conflicts

In a class society such as that of Latin America, every religious activity—
whether it is a matter of ritual, a public statement, or any other religious
function—is carried out (1) by individuals and groups, all of whom are objec-

tively situated in a specific position in the class structure of their society. It is carried out (2) in the sight and presence of other individuals and groups, all of whom are also objectively situated in a particular position in this class society. And it is carried out (3) in conflictive and unequal relationships of power between the diverse classes that constitute this social structure.

To put it another way, in a class society every religious activity is an activity by no means outside or above class conflicts. In a class society every religious activity is an activity carried out within class conflicts, and as such is an activity permeated, limited, and orientated by these conflicts.

But the manner in which such conflicts permeate, limit, and orientate the religious activity taking place in their context varies from one social class to another, and from one social group to another. That is, the objective situation of any individual or group in a determinate position within a class structure disposes them to perceive reality in a manner *corresponding* to their social condition and significantly *opposed* to that of other class positions within the same society.

The leaders and members of any religion in a class society objectively occupy determinate positions in its class structure. This inclines the official representatives of a religion to live and inculcate their religious system in a manner that will vary significantly according to their diverse social conditions. And the manner in which the general public and the membership of a religion will tend to perceive and interpret this religion will likewise significantly vary according to the diverse positions present within society.[66]

And indeed each of the class positions obtaining in a class society implies needs, interests, expectations, customs, thought categories, traditional forms of expression, and behavior patterns that differ from those of any other class position within the same society. Hence the variation, from one social class to another, of the religious undertakings that are possible or impossible, undesirable even though possible, tolerable but only up to a point (a different point in each class), acceptable but just barely, important, basic, or urgent.

These significant variations in the character of a religious activity within a social class—may I be allowed to reemphasize—do not depend so much on the awareness or intentions of religious exponents (or of the public in which the activity is undertaken), but rather on the *objective* position that each sector of the population occupies in the class structure of society.

Consequently, the *rejection* or *acceptance* (and the degree of each) of a religion, its *selective interpretation*, its *propagation* (mass or by sectors, slow or rapid), and its *expressions on the practical level* will vary significantly from one social class to another within the same society at the same time.

Chapter Fifteen

RELIGION IN THE DYNAMICS
OF SOCIAL CLASSES

What we have said thus far about the relationship between religious phenomena and social classes could give the impression that we consider social
classes to be something finished and definitive—static entities. Such is not the
case.

But let us notice in passing that a structural, synchronic, "static" view of
social classes is useful for grasping their reciprocal relationships, for reconstructing the underlying system of social relationships that constitutes certain
human groups in social classes.[67] In so doing, it delimits and orientates the
worldview and practices of such groups.

This static perspective is very useful in the sociological analysis of religions. It can be used for the reconstruction of the articulated set of limitations and orientations that a determinate class society imposes upon the religious activities carried out within it—conditioning their importance, interpretation, propagation, and probable social consequences for each of the
social classes within that society.

But this static perspective, although useful, is not sufficient. Let us move,
then, to a *dynamic* perspective, as we pursue our study of the sociological
aspect of religion that concerns us in Part II—the religious field as a product
of social conflicts.

A social class is a mobile, changing, multiform, and heterogeneous reality
—never simply "given" in static, isolated, definitive form. A social class is
always the *provisional* result of a process inherent in any and every asymmetric mode of production. It results from the tendency to redistribute asymmetrically the members of a determinate community into diverse positions—
positions demanded by the division of labor typifying the particular mode of
production.

But this tendency can be actualized only in and by a *twofold conflictive
process* in the construction of the social classes basic to the mode of production imposed. The conflictive elements of this process are (1) the construction
of such classes from a point of departure in a preliminary situation in which
each of the groups concerned sets up resistance in one way or another to its
relocation in a new division of labor, and (2) the construction of such classes

on a basis of the reduction of massive groups of the population concerned to a situation of subordination. This reduction likewise encounters resistance, variable according to the relative power of the dominant groups in the new mode of production.

In other words, every social class is a group situated in a specific position in the division of labor of a determinate mode of production. It is a group that is defined, limited, and orientated by the position it has in the division of labor, and consequently by the relationships of opposition in which it stands with the other positions constituting such division of labor.

Every social class is also a mobile group, *in process of construction* (or destruction and reconstruction). Its position in the social division of labor is, in every concrete case, a *moment*, or point, of this process of its erection (or dismantling) as a class.

Social Classes and the Religious Field

The relationship of each social class with the religious field of its society comports a multiplicity of aspects that vary from one class to another. There are the needs and interests that preside over its relationship with the religious field. There are its attitudes and preferences with respect to the same. There are its thought categories and its behavioral patterns in this respect. There are its expectations, its de facto awareness, its possible awareness, and so on.

This multiplicity of aspects of the relationship of each social class with the religious field of its society conditions, on the one hand, the type and the orientation of the influence exerted by this social class upon the religious field, and on the other, the selective receptivity that religious activities will encounter within each social class.

Nevertheless every social class is a mobile and heterogeneous group in process of construction, from a point of departure in a preliminary situation. Therefore the relationship of each social class with the religious field at any given historical moment will be determined not only by the structural *position* of this class in the social division of labor—the static perspective—but likewise by the *process* that has brought this particular group to its particular position—the dynamic perspective.

In this sense, then, the relationship of each class fraction with the religious field (and hence its influence on the religious field, and the selective receptivity that it will manifest vis-à-vis the religious activities carried out within it) will be conditioned—over and above its conditioning by the structural *position* of that class—by the following four dimensions of the process of construction of this fraction of a social class.

1. Origin

The particular origin of the class fraction includes the original mode of production (and the place of religion in that mode of production) from which this fraction issues. It includes as well the position the group occupied in this original mode of production (and hence the relationship this fraction had with the religious area in its original mode of production). To be kept in mind is that this origin can go back two or three generations in the history of any given fraction.

2. Trajectory

The class fraction has followed a certain trajectory in the process of its construction, from its origin up to the moment at which it is being studied. This trajectory, if we consider it within a single mode of production, can be ascending, stationary, or descending.[68] In the case of a complex society (one with several modes of production, articulated under the progressive ascendancy of one of them), it is helpful to analyze the trajectory of the fraction in relationship to the dominant mode of production.

The trajectory can, accordingly, be any one of the following:
• Modernization—total incorporation into one of the basic classes of the dominant mode of production.
• Transition—partial incorporation into the dominant mode of production, but without incorporation into any of its basic classes.
• Traditionalism—continuance in a traditional and dominated mode of production.
• Marginalization—a breach with the traditional mode of production, but without achieving incorporation into the dominant mode of production.

In each of these cases it is important to identify the specific trajectory of the particular class fraction with respect to the religious field in particular.

3. Conjuncture

The concrete conjuncture of a particular class fraction is a matter of the concrete relationships of power that, at a determinate moment of its construction as part of a social class, link this fraction with all other social groups of the society. The conjuncture of a class fraction is determined by the relative degree of its class consciousness, its organization as a class, and its capacity for mobilization as a class. (I say "relative" degree because I think this degree should be measured in comparison with these same dimensions in the classes with which the fraction is in alliance or opposition.)

The conjuncture can be considered to be favorable or unfavorable to the class fraction under analysis, depending on whether it facilitates or impedes the attainment of the interests of this fraction at the expense of those of the classes to which it is in opposition. Here it is appropriate to underscore the conjuncture of such a fraction's relationships with the religious field in particular.

4. Strategy

The specific strategy of a class fraction is the fourth and last of the dimensions of the process of class construction that interest us here. By the "strategy" of a class, or fraction of a class, we understand the objective opportunities and tendencies that sketch its probable future in any specific phase—the economic, political, and cultural opportunities and tendencies of this social group. They orientate its thinking and action (independently of the consciousness and will of the persons involved in this strategy).[69]

Strategy—conditioned by the origin, trajectory, position, and relative conjuncture of a given fraction in each concrete case—can therefore be, according to circumstances, that of the acquisition of power, or of the preservation of power acquired, or of protest and demand for reform, or of transactional submission, or of resistance to marginalization.

Hence within the same social *position* and the same social class, there will be a variety of relationships between this class (and its fractions) and the religious field, due to the origin, trajectory, conjuncture, and strategy of this class or fraction. The demands this class makes on the religious field, the degree of influence exerted by these demands on this social field, and the expectations this class or fraction has with respect to religious activities and its selective receptivity to these activities, are therefore conditioned not only by the structural *position* of this social group, but by the dynamic traits of its origin, trajectory, conjuncture, and strategy.[70]

Thus the limitations and orientations to be undergone by a given religion upon contact with the conflictive dynamics of the social classes present will vary from class to class, according to these social dimensions. But, by that very fact, substantial transformations in the conflictive dynamics of these social classes (for instance, in the correlation of forces between the dominating and the dominated in a given period of a society's development) will impose new limitations and orientations upon religions functioning within such classes, constraining these religions to transform themselves (independently of the awareness and desires of their exponents), under pain of stagnation or even extinction.

Hence it is that, sociologically, transformations of the religious field have to be analyzed in the framework of the social conditions in which such transformations have been produced. This is not because all transformations of the religious field always "ought to be" the effect of transformations in social conditions. It is in order to see whether and to what extent these transformations are the mediated product of significant transformations in the conflictive dynamics of social classes.

Chapter Sixteen

RELIGION IN THE DYNAMICS OF CLASS DOMINANCE

The conflictive dynamics inherent in every class society are, in principle, asymmetric. What do we mean by this? We mean, in the first place, that what characterizes a class society as such is precisely the *unequal power* that the various sectors of the division of labor hold over (1) the means of production, (2) the distribution of the work force, and (3) the division of the end products.

In the second place, we mean that the relationships obtaining among the various sectors of the division of labor that constitute the social classes as such are conflictive relationships among unequal forces in a struggle for the control of society. On the one side there are the dominators, attempting to consolidate the power of dominance already in place. On the other side are the dominated, resisting, in various ways, that dominance and striving in some way to increase their own power.

But the dominance of one social class, or bloc of classes, over an entire society is not something that comes about overnight. It is a relatively stable social relationship arising out of a long process of transformation of previous social relationships.[71]

Any social class, or bloc of classes, which, for whatever reasons, is on its way to being constituted as dominant within a society, immediately comes to be located (independently of its consciousness and will) within a *strategy of broadening, deepening, and consolidating the power it has already acquired.*

This strategy—inherent in any class on its way to becoming dominant—will include an interest not only in exercising *coercion*, but also in persuading the dominated classes to give their *consent* to being dominated. Any class on its way to becoming dominant can of course make a beginning simply by using whatever material power (economic, political, military, and so on) it already has that permits it to constrain certain groups to structure themselves socially with a view to the interests of another class. But this constraining class will next be interested in broadening, deepening, and consolidating this material power of coercion.

Power based exclusively on material coercion will be under constant threat of rebellion (especially in the case of colonial enterprises and military dictatorships). Hence any class beginning to dominate will have an interest in matching its material power of *coercion* with a symbolic power of *persuasion*. That is, it will be interested in developing a general consent to its dominance.

In the terminology of Antonio Gramsci, any class beginning to dominate is objectively interested in achieving the establishment of its *hegemony*.[72] Or, in Alain Touraine's terms, any dominant class is interested in becoming the *directing class*—the one that can acquire the massive support of all the classes and groups of society for its specific mode of orientating the control of society.[73]

The strategy of any class on its way to becoming dominant leads it to develop its material power (economic, political, military, and so on), *and* its symbolic power: moral, educational, literary, artistic—and religious.

When a class or bloc of classes is on its way to becoming dominant, its increasing power tends to be exercised more and more over all dimensions of collective life. Its objective is to attain the power of defining, objectively and subjectively, materially and symbolically, the principal *orientations* and basic *limits* of *all* activity carried out within the society in question. To the extent that a class can manage to control access to the principal means of production, the distribution of the greater part of the work force, and the distribution of the basic products of economic activity in a given society, it will have established its material power, however provisionally, over that society. But to the extent that a class has established its material power of dominance over a given society, it will have (1) an *interest* in coordinating all the activities of that society, including religious activities, with a view to broadening, deepening, and consolidating its own dominance. And it will have (2) the *material means* for waging a struggle for the attainment of that interest, with good chances of success.

As a result, any religion in a society where one social class, or bloc of social classes, is on its way to becoming dominant will see itself—progressively and inevitably—subjected to a set of limitations and orientations *generated* by this very process of domination and *tending* to promote not mere dominance, but a deep hegemony.

If the attempt of such a dominant class or bloc to become the governing class is prolonged for several generations, it will have a profound impact on any religions functioning within the society in question. The dynamics of domination can impose itself upon the religious traditions of a population to the point where it (1) *annihilates*, or subjugates, all religious "elements" (belief, rite, behavioral norms, groups, leaders) that appear to constitute an obstacle or danger to its consolidation of power. It (2) *favors* the creation or development of all religious elements clearly converging toward consolidation of power by the dominant class. And it (3) *restructures*, more in line with the new situation of dominance, all religious elements not presenting a direct obstacle to consolidation of power by the dominant class.[74]

In this context we must emphasize that the *reading* of the foundational proclamation of any religion, as well as its *interpretation*, and the ethical, liturgical, doctrinal, and organizational *definitions* deriving from such interpretation, are—always—taken, worked out, and propagated in the framework of a specific society, and of a particular structure of power relationships among the groups forming the society. When the society is a class society, the dynamics of domination imposes its *limitations* and *orientations* even upon the reading, the interpretation, and the official definitions deriving from the foundational proclamation of that religion.

Often this process translates into a religious universalization and sacralization of mental structures that properly speaking are to be found neither in the foundational message, nor in the interpretation of that message by the religious functionaries charged with such interpretation, nor even in the audience to whom that interpretation is addressed. Rather, these mental structures originate primarily in the dominant classes of the society in which this process is occurring.[75]

This process of the subjection of the religious field to the dynamics of class dominance is the result of the *objective* interest of the dominant classes in achieving consolidation of their domination and the establishment of their hegemony. This process does not depend on the awareness or desires or intention of the social agents of the dominant classes. Nor does the subjection of the religious field to these dynamics of dominance depend on any awareness on the part of its exponents. On the contrary: the effort to subject the religious field to the dynamics of class dominance will be all the more efficacious if there is no explicit consciousness of the process at work, which is what generally happens.

Chapter Seventeen

RELIGION IN THE DYNAMICS OF CLASS RESISTANCE TO DOMINANCE

No class society is a society of pure dominance. Dominance is exercised over individuals and groups who dispose of only a bare minimum of power over any means of production, over distribution of even their own labor, and over the division of the end products of their labor. But these individuals and groups, though generally unarmed, are never altogether inert. Faced with dominance, the dominated always, somehow, offer *resistance*.

A social group does not become dominated overnight. Even when it passes from a situation of traditional subordination to a new type of subordination (for example, when landless peasants become sharecroppers) every dominated social group comes to occupy its position through a *process*. Such a process of subjection is, always, a conflictive process, full of reversals and stagnations. If the process results in a dominated group it will only be because this group lacked the power, material or symbolic, to halt or reverse the process.

Any social group on its way to becoming a dominated group adopts a *strategy of resistance to dominance*—independently of its consciousness and will.

For their part, the dominant classes, even in the apparently most stable phase of consolidation of their hegemony, never attain to an absolute control over collective life. There always remains a certain resistance on the part of the dominated—even if only in the form of silence, confusion, noncooperation, hysteria, or purely destructive terror.

Of course, the resistance of the dominated often takes the form of a search for compensation rather than conscious and organized collective rebellion, especially at moments when their routes to liberation seem blocked. But resistance there is, and it comes into conflict with the strategy of the dominators.

The conflict *manifests* itself as conflict only at tense moments of collective life, such as times of crisis and sudden change. But in one way or another the

75

resistance of the dominated tends to take shape (and this is precisely what makes them dominated) within the limits and orientations imposed by the dominating classes (which is precisely what makes them dominant).[76]

At the same time, any social group that is dominated—or on its way to being dominated—imposes *specific limitations and orientations* upon activities arising within its own ambit—limitations and orientations distinct from, and in certain cases even directly opposed to, those of the dominant classes. Thus religious activities performed within the dominated classes, however influenced by dominant limitations and orientations, will to some extent be penetrated, limited, and specially orientated by the origin, trajectory, position, conjuncture, and strategy of the dominated classes themselves.

There is one aspect of the conflictive dynamics of resistance to domination on the part of subordinate classes that, from the viewpoint of the sociologist of religion, is deserving of special attention. It is the interest of the dominated class in achieving the maximum possible autonomy vis-à-vis the dominant classes. This tendential autonomy is expressed not only at the level of production, but at the symbolic level as well—the cultural level. The interest entertained by every dominated class in achieving maximal *autonomy* is in direct conflict with the interest of every dominating class to establish its *hegemony*.

This objective interest of the subordinate classes in achieving maximal autonomy, material and symbolic, vis-à-vis the dominating classes includes a certain tendency to achieve a *religious autonomy*. That is, it involves a tendency to construct a system of religious thought and practices that favor the subordinate classes' objective interests. Hence all religious agents—whether organizations, ministers, or preachers—performing a religious activity within the subordinate classes will be subjected to a certain limitation and orientation of their activity by this interest of the dominated to achieve religious autonomy.

The result of the process will partially depend upon the objective relationships of power in the hands of the dominated with respect to the dominating —that is, upon the relative degree of class consciousness, organization, and mobilization of the opposing classes or bloc of classes. It will also depend upon the origin, trajectory, and strategy of the dominated classes. The concrete result will be anything from the simple creation of a specific (dominated) tendency of the subordinate classes within the predominant religious system, without shocks or breaches in the religious field, to the massive conversion of broad subordinate sectors to sects or religious movements partially autonomous with respect to the predominant religious system.[77]

In all cases the interest of the subordinate classes in achieving a religious autonomy will always have a significant impact on the structuring and dynamics of the religious field. Whatever the nature and degree of that impact, the conflict between the opposing interests of *autonomy* on the part of the dominated and *hegemony* on that of the dominating will translate into a latent or open conflict in the religious field between the religious agents espousing these respective tendencies. By way of corollary, the seeming unity enjoyed by certain religious systems (monopolistic churches, for example) in class societies will be constantly under threat of conflict, schism, and sectarian movements, in resonance with conflict between the dominating and the dominated.

The force of the impact of each of the various dominated classes upon the religious field, as well as the degree of transformation that the interest of each of these classes in its religious autonomy can provoke in the religious field, is something that will vary significantly among dominated classes. The impact and transformation will be significantly greater, for example, in the case of subordinate classes whose traits (origin, trajectory, demographic proportion, position, conjuncture, strategy, and so on) mark them as *revolutionary classes*—that is, as classes objectively and subjectively capable of generating a social movement orientated toward a radical transformation of the established social order.

By contrast, the impact of these classes and the changes they can generate in the religious field will be only of minimal significance in cases where their traits mark them as *purely dominated classes*—classes objectively and subjectively incapable of developing as autonomous classes (with class consciousness, organization, and mobilization). Hence they are incapable of seriously threatening the power of the dominant classes of their society.

To conclude, we posit the following hypothesis: class resistance to domination will impose its own orientations and limitations upon the reading, interpretation, and official definitions of the foundational message of any religion operating within subordinate classes.[78]

PART III

Religion as a Relatively Autonomous Terrain of Social Conflicts

Part II represents an attempt to delineate a sociological approach to a single aspect of the relationships between social conflicts and the religious field. Which aspect? That of the religious field as *product* of social conflicts.

We have seen how social conflicts—particularly in Latin America as a result of the transformations and successive situations of domination that have taken place there—exert a decisive influence on the religions functioning in a society, any society, by limiting and orientating their activity. They condition the importance, the interpretation, the propagation, the mutations, the organization, and the ritual and discursive production of those religions.

Even from the strictly sociological viewpoint that we are attempting to develop here, the complex relationship of the religious field to social conflicts is *not* reducible to the influence of the latter over the former. The religious field is not merely a product of social conflicts. Besides being (partially) the product of social conflicts, the religious field is something else as well, something more. (In fact, even in its quality as product of social conflicts, the religious field is something more. It is not the inert and passive product of such conflicts.)

In Part III we shall pursue the development of the theoretical framework we have drawn up for the analysis of the interrelationships of the religious field with social conflicts in Latin America. But it will be *another* aspect of these interrelationships that we shall be examining. Now we shall see the religious field in its sociological specificity, in its own proper dynamics.

We shall concentrate on the sociological fact of the religious field as a social field having an activity that is (partially) its own particular activity. That is, we shall concentrate on the *autonomy* of religion. At the same time we shall not forget what we have already seen: that the religious area is always situated in a determinate social context that limits and orientates it, and hence renders the specific autonomy of religion *relative* to that context.

The religious area, as we shall see, is not only a product of macrosocial relationships and conflicts. It also constitutes, by itself, a specific network of microsocial relationships with a certain reality and stability of its own. We shall now undertake an analysis of the internal relationships of the religious field—and more particularly of the microsocial conflicts generated within this social field. They constitute its principal dynamics.[79] And we shall do so from the perspective of Latin America's problems today.

Chapter Eighteen

RELIGIOUS INTEREST AND RELIGIOUS PRODUCTION

Every person, as also every human collectivity, is interested in—or better still, has a need for[80]—having a communicable representation of their natural and social surroundings that will permit them to take a position and perform an activity within their milieu.

Without a representation of the world to structure a collective experience of natural and social surroundings, the survival of the individual or collectivity becomes practically impossible. And it is only a *socially shared* representation of the world that will make survival possible for human beings.

Such a representation of the world—subjected repeatedly to unforeseen exigencies, which will of course demand that it be modified again and again, partially or totally—is built up by putting together associations, dissociations, and oppositions among the elements of past and present experience shared by the social group in question. The associations, dissociations, and oppositions are put together through the mediation of various languages, verbal as well as nonverbal.

Thus there arises a concrete system of communicable representations, which define—for a determinate community and in particular circumstances —what is possible or impossible, useful, irrelevant, or prejudicial, desirable or undesirable, forbidden, permitted, or obligatory, important, secondary, or indifferent, changeable or unchangeable, deniable or undeniable, urgent or deferrable, and so on.

We shall not explore the thesis—which goes far beyond the purview of the social sciences—that every individual has an intrinsic need to represent the world in a religious manner.[81] Instead we shall begin with what appears to be an incontrovertible sociological fact—namely, that some societies—and in others, certain social groups, for reasons that are not yet clear[82] and are not to our purpose to discuss here—construct worldviews with a central or lateral reference to supernatural and metasocial forces, on which they feel dependent, and before which they consider themselves obligated to certain conduct. In a word, some societies and some social groups tend to develop a *religious worldview*, whether totally or partially religious.

Religious Interest

In these societies or social fractions, an interest in the collective sharing of a worldview permitting them to situate and orientate themselves in their natural and social ambient translates into the specific interest that the representation of the world refer *clearly* and *directly* to supernatural and metasocial forces. In other words, in societies and social groups whose worldview tends to be religious, the interest in having a communicable representation of their milieu that will permit them to situate themselves in it and to act in it is defined as a *specifically religious interest.*

"Religious interest" can therefore be defined as that need, present in some societies and some social groups, to situate and orientate themselves—and to act—in their natural and social milieu *through the mediation of* a view of this milieu that is referred—centrally or laterally, totally or partially—to metasocial and supernatural forces upon which the group feels dependent and before which it considers itself obligated to a certain conduct.

A specifically religious interest moves its subjects to make an effort to develop a religious worldview that will permit them to situate and orientate themselves—and to act—in the most satisfactory manner possible in the natural and social milieu in which they happen to live. The effort to develop such a worldview—the effort motivated by this religious interest—is what we shall call the *work of specifically religious production.*

Religious Production

All religious work, it would seem, owes its origin to the collective experience of some charismatic personality.[83] Mere religious interest, in and of itself, seems somehow inadequate to set in motion a process of religious production. Such interest can long remain in an unsatisfied state or collective malaise (perhaps no more than a generation, however, without provoking a collective crisis). In order that a religious interest issue in the work of religious production, it seems necessary that there be a collective experience of a charismatic personality—a person or group incarnating, in words and deeds, elements capable of initiating a social process of religious production.

To the extent that a religious interest impels a society or social group to represent the world through the mediation of religious work—whose intellectual component is, as we see, basic—to this extent religious work is *subjective.* And to the extent that the subjects of a religious interest are social groups formed by individuals—individuals who are the "depositories" of that representation of the world to which such religious interest impels its subjects—to this extent the religious work has an *individual* character.

But religious work is never either purely subjective or exclusively individual. Religious work is always *collective* work, as well. This is the case from several points of view. Religious work is performed by a collectivity of human beings directly or indirectly participating in the development of a world-view toward which their religious interest is tendentially directed (likewise making it a collective interest). The worldview also has a role in making possible the appearance of the charismatic personality of a founder (situated in a social context).

The raw material of such work is a *general* collective experience (of usages and customs, beliefs, traditions, norms, relationships, successes and failures, and so on), accumulated over several generations. It also is the *particular* collective experience of a charismatic personality.

Similarly the instruments of this religious work—language, first of all—are instruments transformed and used collectively. Then, the product of this religious work can be such only to the extent that it is shared by the collectivity to which it is directed. Finally, the purpose for which such work is intended, whether or not this purpose is actually achieved, is a social one—that of preserving or transforming a determinate situation (internal or external) of the collectivity that is the subject of the religious interest.

In other words, religious work, notwithstanding its individual aspect, is *socially productive work*.

But religious work is likewise *objective*. And here again, this is true in several senses.[84] It is work performed by objectively existent human beings—just as the work's founder was also someone objectively existent. Then, a great part of the raw material of this work consists in objectively crystalized collective experience: material symbols (oral, written, iconographic, gestural), organized units of space, and observable, systematized behavior.

Similarly, some of the instruments of religious work have objective reality: teachings, ritual, sacred space, vestments, objects of devotion, and the like. Then too the product of religious work is never merely a subjective worldview. As the communicable and shared worldview it seeks to be, the product of religious work has an objective facet: texts, verbal formulas, perceptible and patterned conduct, an institutionalized use of space and time, and so on.

Finally, religious work, in its character as a socially productive process generated by the specifically religious interest of certain communities and groups, is directed toward an objective social function: the enablement of the collective subject of that religious interest to act in its socio-natural ambient for the preservation or transformation of its objective situation within that ambient.

In short, as well as being subjective, religious work is *objectively productive work*.

In saying all this we have no wish to seem to minimize the individual and subjective character of religious work. On the contrary, it seems to us indisputable that religious work has an important individual and subjective aspect.[85] We are focusing here on the social and objective aspect of religious work simply because it is only under this aspect that religious work can form the object of sociology.

By way of synthesis, we may state that religion, any religion, is not only or primarily a given, already structured set of characteristics and doctrine referring to supernatural and metasocial forces. No, religion, any religion, is the *result of a productive process.* It is the product of a socially objective work of structuring the collective experience of a community, from a point of departure in contact with a charismatic personality, and based on an interest in having a worldview with a reference to supernatural, metasocial forces.

Religion, any religion, before it can crystalize into a system of doctrine and practices having a reference to supernatural and metasocial forces—that is, before it is a *product*—is a *production process.*

Chapter Nineteen

CONSTITUTION OF A FIELD SPECIALIZING IN RELIGIOUS PRODUCTION

As Pierre Bourdieu has observed, societies can be classified according to their degree of specialization of religious work—from societies in which there is practically no such specialization (societies in which all members of the community participate more or less equally in religious production) to societies in which religious work is the monopoly of a stable body of functionaries specializing in this work.[86]

The greater or lesser possibility of specialization in religious work depends, as we have already observed, on the greater or lesser degree of division of the general work of the collectivity in question. But above all it seems to be with urbanization, the ensuing dissociation and opposition of city and countryside, and the concentration of intellectual tasks in urban centers (alongside the tasks of direction and control of production and commerce) that religious work, also concentrated in the cities, reaches its maximal differentiation and specialization.

Specialization of religious work means that religious production is no longer something engaged in indiscriminately by each and all the members of a community. That is, the work of religious production becomes a differentiated productive task, within the labor collective, assigned to a particular group within the community—a group which basically specializes in this task. Its survival (through the mediation of the goods necessary for *its own* subsistence, goods produced by *other* groups) depends on the execution of its specific contribution to the benefit of the rest of the community.

That contribution consists in the satisfaction of the religious interest of the social groups that are the subjects of that interest—that is, on the production of a communicable worldview, with a reference to supernatural and metasocial forces, which will permit such groups to situate and orientate themselves, and to act, in the most satisfactory manner possible within their natural and social milieu.

Briefly, then, specialization of religious work consists in the gradual establishment of a *body of functionaries* specifically charged with satisfying a particular type of interest (the religious interest) characteristic of certain social groups, by way of the development (religious production) of a certain type of teaching and practices (religious teaching and practices).

In Latin America, as we have seen, Luso-Hispanic colonialism established a marked social division of labor. Similarly, religious work was gradually established as specialized work, assigned to a body of functionaries (the Catholic clergy), concentrated in urban centers. As in Europe in an earlier age, this new development constituted a landmark in the history of Latin America. With the appearance of a body of functionaries specializing in religious production, religion was now no longer a product arising directly out of the interest of indigenous Latin American communities. Little by little, undifferentiated religious activity, carried out in indissoluble linkage with the total activity of the indigenous communities,[87] gave way to the genesis of a religious field—an articulated complexus of individuals, groups, and institutions specially charged with satisfying the religious interest of the various groups comprising Latin American societies.

The constitution of a religious field in any society establishes a special sociological situation for the further development of religious teaching and practices in that society. As we observed in Part II, the *internal division of religious work* generally ensuing upon the establishment of a body of functionaries specializing in religious production creates a set of socio-religious conditions that limit and orientate religious work in a manner radically distinct from the situation of an unspecialized religious production.

The type and degree of the internal division of religious work condition the type of organization that will have the best chances of development within the religious field, as well as its degree of diversification. They will likewise condition the type of practices that more probably will be institutionalized in the religious area, as well as the degree of their bureaucratization. Finally, they will condition the type of discourse that more probably will be propagated in the religious field, as well as the degree of its systemization and moralization.

In other words, it is the type and degree of *internal* division of the specific work of the religious field, and *not* the social structure directly, that will have the more immediate influence on the possibility or impossibility, the desirability or undesirability, the acceptance and the limits of acceptance, the relevance or irrelevance, and the urgency or nonurgency of any religious organization, teaching, or practice, as well as certain internal characteristics of such organizations, teachings, and practices.

Thus the concrete traits characterizing the religious field in a determinate society will constitute the focus of *limitations* and *orientations* most directly, specifically, and immediately restricting and directing the rise, propagation, and transformations of religious activities in that society.

The religious field, precisely as the complexus of social agents and institutions specially charged with religious production, constitutes the mediating instance of the impact of social conflict upon religious production as such. In this capacity the religious field can impede, facilitate, filter selectively, or orientate influences arising *outside* the religious field but nevertheless tending to be exercised *upon* the religious area.

Relative Autonomy of the Religious Field

It is in this sense, among others, that we speak of a *relative autonomy* of the religious field—namely, in the sense in which structures, conflicts, and transformations occurring on the level of an entire society as such do *not* directly, mechanically, or automatically influence religious teachings and practices within that society.[88]

Further, the effect that such structures, struggles, and mutations (occurring at the level of a whole society as such) can have on religious teachings and practices within that society is a *variable* effect. It is variable not only according to extrareligious circumstances (as we saw in Part II), but according to *internal* conditions of the religious field as well. That is, the tendential effect of social structures, struggles, and transformations upon religious teachings and practices is a *mediate* effect—mediated by the religious field as such— and a *variable* effect—dependent on the internal situation of the religious field.

When we say that the religious field is relatively autonomous, we mean that this field is *neither absolutely independent* with respect to social structures, conflicts, and transformations (as we have already seen) *nor totally determined* by these structures, conflicts, and transformations. Or, to state it positively, the religious field is *partially conditioned* by social structures, conflicts, and transformations, but is also *partially independent* in their regard —hence relatively autonomous.

The basis of the (relative) autonomy of any religion, religious system, or structured complexus of religious teachings and practices—and *a fortiori* the basis of the (relative) autonomy of the religious area—is, sociologically speaking, threefold:

1. Subjective Dimension

Every religious system has a subjective dimension. After all, a religious system entails a *worldview* capable of satisfactorily orientating a community or social group in its socio-natural milieu. In this sense every socially shared religious system becomes an interiorized, introjected system for the believers within it.

This internalization or introjection of a religious system on the part of a social group offers this religious system a certain autonomy and continuity— a certain *psycho-social* consistency—that will render the group resistant to sudden and repeated transformations. It thereby generates a tendency to perpetuate the religious system. Thus we can speak of a certain subjective *psycho-social* basis for the (relative) autonomy of any religion.

2. Objective Dimension

Every religious system has an objective dimension as well. After all, a religious system entails a set of socially shared *teachings* and *practices*. This objectivization in a structured set of teachings and practices shared and repeated by a community or social group also offers any religious system a certain autonomy and continuity—a certain *social* consistency. It too will contribute to rendering the system resistant to sudden and repeated transformations. And it will strengthen the tendency to the self-perpetuation of that system.[89]

3. Institutional Dimension

Finally, as we saw above, certain religious systems have an institutional dimension properly so called. After all, a religious system is produced, reproduced, preserved, and propagated by a stable body of organized functionaries.

This institutionalization of certain religious systems offers them a still greater autonomy and continuity—a greater *microsocial* consistency. This will contribute to rendering them still more resistant to repeated and sudden transformations, further consolidating the tendency of any religious system toward self-perpetuation.[90]

Chapter Twenty

RISE OF CONFLICTS INVOLVING RELIGIOUS PRODUCTION

The positioning of a body of functionaries specifically charged with satisfying the religious interest of certain social groups by the production of a certain type of teachings and practices—or more briefly, the specialization of religious work—issues from a conflictive process.

A social group whose religious work has traditionally been undifferentiated will tend to protect this mode of religious production from any sudden transformation. That is, it will tend autonomously and continuously to adhere to its own mode of religious evolvement. By that very fact, the attempt to substitute a new mode of religious production for the traditional one—the attempt to introduce a mode in which religious production will be partially or totally monopolized by a body of functionaries specializing in religious work—will encounter resistance and rejection in the community concerned.

Resistance and rejection will be greater in cases where the initiative for modification of the mode of the community's religious production will have come *from without*. And they will be greater still if this initiative will have been accompanied by the attempt to *modify other aspects* of the life of the community as well—for example, economic, political, military, linguistic, or educational aspects.

For these reasons among others, the establishment and consolidation of a body of functionaries specializing in religious work implies a parallel process of *expropriation of the means of religious production*. That is, in order for a group to be able to set itself up as a body specializing in religious production within a community traditionally characterized by undifferentiated religious activity, it will be necessary for this group to come to grips with the collective resistance and the tendencies to perpetuate the traditional mode of religious production.

In this struggle, the emergent group interested in monopolizing religious production will have a tendency to dispossess the community of its means of religious production—sacred places, objects of devotion, ritual formulas, organization of religious time, and so on. This dispossession or expropriation of the means of religious production will be followed either by a *private appropriation* of these means by the emerging group or by the partial or total *annihilation* of these means of production, joined to the partial or total *substitution* for these means of production by other means already in the hands of the emergent group.

If this expropriation of the means of religious production does not succeed in overcoming the resistance of the community concerned, the result of the struggle can range from the elimination of the emergent group to its survival as a minority religious sect within the community. In all cases, failure in the attempt to overcome community resistance by expropriation of its means of production will prevent the establishment of a body of functionaries that can monopolize religious production in the community.

If, on the contrary, the attempt at expropriation of a community's means of religious production succeeds, the result will be the formation of a body of functionaries ("clergy," in a broad sense). It will be partially or totally the *proprietor* of the principal legitimate means of religious production in the community. The remaining members of the community will become the *dispossessed* (the "laity," in a broad sense), forced to have recourse to the clergy in order to satisfy their religious interest.

The success or failure of a struggle to dispossess a community of its means of religious production depends on various factors. On the one hand, of course, there are *extrareligious* social factors, especially the material force at the disposition of each of the groups in conflict over the directioning of religious evolvement. For example, one reason among others why the Catholic Church was able to impose itself in Latin America was that it could count on the economic, political, juridical, and military support of the Spanish and Portuguese thrones. This support was far superior to the resources of the Latin American Indians.

On the other hand, the success or failure of this type of struggle depends on factors properly *socio-religious* as well. This could be, for example, any antecedent religious dissatisfaction on the part of the community, combined with the rise of a charismatic personality within an emergent group seeking the monopolization of religious production.

Expropriation can take variable, diverse, and in many instances complementary forms, all depending on the situation. They can range from violent preemption to reasoned persuasion, by the introduction of new and more attractive forms of piety. Between these extremes are competition, the substitution for or conversion of traditionally communitarian means of religious productivity in favor of their private application at the hands of emergent clergy, and so on.

To cite but one example in detail, an emergent clergy can expropriate a traditionally communitarian religious ritual such as the invocation of supernatural forces to obtain rain by recourse to a number of strategies:

• *Disqualification*—designating the traditional rite "sorcery."

• *Conversion*—crediting the occurrence of rain to a religious figure strange to the community but familiar to the emergent clergy.

- *Disparagement*—announcing the exact date when rains should begin and, when drought continues, denouncing the inefficacy of the traditional religious practice.
- *Replacement*—introducing another rite, showier and more emotionally satisfying.
- *Competition*—introducing a new rite, controlled by the emergent clergy, celebrated during and after the rains.
- In extreme cases, violent *persecution* of the traditional rite.

Several of these modalities can be combined, to yield a greater efficacy in the particular *strategy of expropriation* an emerging clergy must wield in a community having a tradition of undifferentiated religious practice.

May we emphasize again that a process of this sort is independent of the conscious intentions of religious exponents. It is the *objective placement* within a community of a body of functionaries specializing in religious production, *not* the *subjective intentions* of a clergy, that principally determines the genesis of the tendency to expropriate the means of religious production.

The mere fact that a strategy of expropriation has been successful does not mean that a religious sphere free of antagonisms will result. On the contrary, to the extent that any religious system has a subjective dimension, to this same extent the traditional religious system, dispossessed of its own means of development, will tend to continue in latent form. It will tend to be passed on—however submissive and dominated—offering resistance to attempts at its annihilation. It will have an unconscious or clandestine existence. It bears within it conflictive potentialities that may openly erupt when the religious field least expects it.

Of course, to the extent that a specialization in religious work results from an objective, and not merely subjective, imposition, to this same extent resistance against it can be reduced. Struggle against this resistance can be institutionalized. But the conflict that has established the distinct religious field, though dormant, does not disappear.

Chapter Twenty-One

CONFLICTIVE FRAGMENTATION OF RELIGIOUS INTEREST AND WORK

The appearance of a specialized body of functionaries charged with productive religious work, together with the correlative formation of a distinct religious field and the constitution of the greater part of the members of the community as a "laity" (objectively dispossessed of the principal legitimate means of religious production), constitutes the first great *division of religious work*.

Rarely, however, does the division of religious work end with the simple differentiation of the categories "clergy" and "laity." Generally the religious field tends to reproduce within itself the principal hierarchical schemata and categories of a class-society division of labor. The placement of a body of functionaries specializing in religious work makes this possible (and almost inevitable). This occasions a deeper (and conflictive) internal division of religious work.

In this same order of ideas, we can point out that what may have been a single common religious interest in small societies with a communitarian mode of production, now, in asymmetric societies with a specialization of religious work, becomes a *set of conflictively and asymmetrically structured religious interests*. In asymmetric societies with a specialization of religious work, this fragmentation of religious interest operates at three distinct and complementary levels.

1. Division of Clergy and Laity

The religious interest of the clergy becomes, in the first instance, an interest in preserving, extending, and deepening its power over the production, reproduction, exchange, and distribution of *religious goods* (i.e., the means of salvation) and accordingly its power over the means of religious production.

The religious interest of the laity, in opposition and subordination to the clergy, becomes an interest in restraining, and if possible reversing, the process of expropriation of the means of religious production. That is, the interest of the laity becomes, as a minimum, an interest in obtaining religious goods with minimal concessions to the clergy. As a maximum, it seeks a re-appropriation of the means of religious production in their totality. This is the first asymmetric and conflictive fragmentation of religious interest.

2. Internal Division of the Laity

The religious interest of the laity becomes a *religious demand* directed toward the clergy. To the extent that the laity comprises a public formed of social fractions objectively situated in opposing positions and having the mutual relationships set up by dominance, to this same extent the religious interests of the lay public will be conflictively and asymmetrically organized in a constellation of differentiated and even opposing religious demands.

To cite merely the most general and best known opposition characteristic of the lay public, we note with Max Weber that these demands will be organized around two fundamental poles. There will be the pole of the dominant classes, whose religious demand will tend toward a worldview that will permit them to continue to situate and orientate themselves, and to act, as dominant. That is, their religious interest will be defined as a demand for the *legitimation of dominance.* And there will be the pole of the dominated classes, whose religious demand will tend toward a worldview that will permit them either to compensate for or to reverse their subordinate situation. That is, their religious interest will be defined in the area between a demand for *compensation of their subordinate condition* and a *demand for reversal of the legitimation of the established order.*

This is the second asymmetric and conflictive fragmentation of religious interest.

3. Internal Division of the Clergy

The religious interest of the clergy as such inclines to the acquisition and preservation of religious power. But the (conflictive and asymmetric) diversity of socially objective origins, trajectories, and positions, within and without the religious field, of each and all the individuals and groups constituting the clergy, also issues, generally, in a conflict, at least a latent one, among the different categories of religious functionaries. This conflict translates into a diversity of strategies for the acquisition and preservation of religious power. It can range from transactional ("negotiated") convergence to a breach with the institution.

Simultaneously, the reproduction of hierarchical superiors and categories of social division of labor within the religious field itself, combined with what we have seen in the division of the laity discussed just above, determines a structuring of the clergy as a body with internal *relationships of religious domination*. These relationships make the clergy to be an area of conflict—conflict between those who retain greater religious power, and those who carry out the work of production and reproduction of religious goods in subordination to them. The "higher clergy" is interested in preserving, extending, and deepening its acquired religious power. The "lower clergy" is interested rather in acquiring a greater proportion of this religious power, which it shares only in subordination (having greater power, however, than the laity).

This is the third and last asymmetric and conflictive fragmentation of religious interest that we need to consider.

Internal division of religious work, with its consequent fragmentation of religious interest into a structure of *multiple, diverse, opposing, and asymmetrical religious interests,* leads to a complex *structure of internal dominance* in the religious area.

In this (conflictive and asymmetric) structure of religious dominance, a first relationship of dominance is that between clergy and laity. The clergy appropriates the means of religious production, of which the laity are dispossessed. But within this relationship—and within the clergy itself—there is a second relationship of religious dominance, one between higher and lower clergy. The higher clergy retains *proprietorship* over the means of religious productivity, while the lower clergy retains only *use* of the same (that is, the authorization to make use of such means, and to manage the corresponding production, only to the extent authorized by the proprietors)—and, to be sure, not of all of them.[91]

The double conflict (between clergy and laity, and higher clergy and lower clergy) latent in a religious structure of domination as here described, has enormously significant implications for the religious *organization, practices,* and *theorization* produced within that structure. Apart from a necessary *diversification* of religious activity in these three dimensions, as a consequence of a conflictive and asymmetric fragmentation of religious interest, a *systematization* and *moralization* of religious thinking becomes necessary— and thereby a systematization and moralization of the practices and organization pertaining to this theorization.

Systematization consists in the constitution of the production of religious discourse as a *unified and coherent* production, with a view to the symbolic reduction of the conflicts latent in the religious field, in order thereby to hamper their development and eruption. Moralization consists in a systematic emphasis on the production, reproduction, and inculcation of *norms of conduct* (prohibitions, obligations, rights, and so on) tending to stabilize and sacralize the relationships of religious domination, and thereby to avoid any rebellion against the established order.[92]

The result is that, with the specialization and internal division of religious work, religious production will not only have the extrainstitutional function of satisfying the religious interest of certain social groups. It will also have the *intrainstitutional* function of preserving an (unstable and asymmetric) equilibrium within the religious field itself.

Chapter Twenty-Two

RELIGIOUS PRODUCTION AS TRANSACTIONAL PRODUCTION

In its quality as complexus of religious agents and institutions in inter-action, the religious field is, as we have seen, characterized by a structure of asymmetric and conflictive interests articulated in a double relationship of dominance.

In societies with a sector of agents and institutions specializing in religious work, religious production (discursive as well as ritual and organizational) is subjected to a set of unequal and opposed demands. They exert pressure on that production, limiting and orientating its development.

The religious field must satisfy the respective interests of each category of clergy as well as those of each fraction of the laity. Production carried on by the religious field will tend precisely to the satisfaction of the (asymmetric and conflictive) interests of each category of clergy and each fraction of the corresponding lay audience. A prolonged absence of satisfaction of the spe-cific religious interest of a particular category of clergy can issue in the devel-opment and eruption of an intrareligious conflict (e.g., the Lefebvre case). In certain circumstances it can occasion the defection of that particular cate-gory of clergy and the formation of a new religious system in competition with the one traditionally dominating the field (e.g., the case of the Old Catholics). A prolonged absence of satisfaction of the specific religious in-terest of a particular fraction of the laity, for its part, can issue in the massive defection of a group of the faithful and its emigration to a dominated reli-gious system, strengthening it and consequently weakening the dominant re-ligious system.

Inasmuch, then, as the categories of clergy holding power in a religious system have an interest directly opposed to any breach and defection on the part of clergy as well as laity, the general tendency that will limit and orientate production in the religious field will be precisely the satisfaction of the in-terests of each category of clergy and each fraction of the laity in the religious field in question.

We have already observed that the interests of the different categories of

95

clergy are conflictive—mutually opposed. Hence it is impossible *totally* to satisfy the interests of each and every category of clergy constituting the religious area. Besides, as we have seen, these interests are not only conflictive, they are also asymmetric. For inasmuch as the conflict in question is waged in and through a relationship of dominance, the ability of each category of clergy to impose its own interests depends upon whether it is a dominant or a dominated category. Accordingly, it is impossible for religious production to be orientated to the *equal* satisfaction of the interests of each and every category of clergy.

As a consequence, the conflictive and asymmetric character of the religious interests of the different categories of clergy will orientate religious production toward a *partial* and *unequal* satisfaction of such interests. Each category will have to accept, at least provisionally, the nonsatisfaction of part of its interests, in exchange for the satisfaction of another part of its interests. But of course the categories of clergy that dominate will generally achieve greater satisfaction of their interests than the subordinate clergy.

Something analogous occurs with the various fractions of the laity. To the extent that its religious interests, as well, are, both mutually and with respect to the religious interests of the clergy, *conflictive* and *asymmetric,* a *total* and *equal* satisfaction of the religious interests of each and every one of the social fractions constituting the laity will be impossible. Hence the religious field will have to orientate its production toward a *partial* and *unequal* satisfaction of the religious interests of each of the social fractions of the lay audience. The dominant social fractions will receive, or tend to receive, a greater, though incomplete, satisfaction of their religious demands, whereas the subordinate classes will receive a lesser, and incomplete, satisfaction of their demands.

Furthermore, it is clear that the clergy, on the whole, will satisfy its own religious needs incompletely, but generally to a greater extent than the laity, on the whole.

We may summarize, then, by saying that religious production developed in a class society with specialized religious work is always a *transactional religious production.* That is, it is a production that, by reason of its effectuation in a milieu of multiple, diverse, conflictive, and asymmetric interests, tends to satisfy each and all of the different categories and fractions interested in this production in a *partial* and *unequal* manner (in the form of unconscious negotiation—a tacit *do ut des* contract).

The dynamics of the religious field—that is, its activity and the transformations of that activity—will be based precisely on the inevitable conflicts, and correlative transactions, arising (1) out of the diversity of interests *between clergy and laity,* and (2) out of the diversity of interests *among the different categories of clergy.*

The reason why the religious field's production of discourse, practices, and organization of a religious type is constant is that it operates in the constant presence of partially unsatisfied religious interests, whose subjects exert pressure on this religious field to achieve greater satisfaction of these interests.

But the reason why religious production varies from one age to another and from one set of circumstances to another is precisely that the relationships of power between clergy and laity, and the relationships of competition among the different categories of clergy, are relationships characterized by an unstable equilibrium. It is an equilibrium that tends constantly to dissolve and re-form, thereby modifying the concrete conditions in which religious interests compete for satisfaction.

There is a third basic element of the dynamics of the religious area, besides the two we have indicated in the paragraphs just above. This element is (3) the diversity of interests *among the different fractions of the laity.*

Nevertheless we have to observe in this connection that the activity of the social structure (that is, the activity of the social fractions that are mutually opposed by relationships of dominance) upon the dynamics of the religious field is never an *immediate* activity. This is never the case.

The social structure acts upon the dynamics of the religious field (that is, upon the activity and transformations of specialized religious production) through the *mediation* of the religious demands corresponding to each social class or fraction thereof. In their turn, these demands do not penetrate the religious area "directly," so to speak. They are transmitted to the interior of the religious area through categories of clergy in contact with the social fraction concerned in each concrete case.[93]

Thus the internal situation of the religious field in each specific *religious conjuncture* will mediate in a peculiar manner the demands of the social agents in conflict. In each concrete religious conjuncture, there will be a determinate set of possibilities and impossibilities, apertures and blockages, facing the religious demands of the laity. They will limit and orient the specific form and content of production tending *transactionally* (that is, partially and unequally) to satisfy these demands.

Notwithstanding all that we have said, a tendency is to be noted in the religious field for the dominant clerical categories to identify with the socially dominant fractions. A sort of reciprocal "understanding" and support arises between the two groups. This tendency derives, among other reasons, from the structural homology of the respective (dominant) positions of these groups. It derives as well from the fact that the social origin of the higher clergy is generally to be found in socially dominant fractions.

For these and other reasons, there exists a tendency to a sort of identification between the two groups, just as there also exists a tendency, a weaker one, to a sort of identification between the subordinate categories of the clergy and the socially subordinate fractions of the laity. These identifications generate, at the level of the religious field, a set of differentiated sensitivities and restraints among the various categories of clergy vis-à-vis the different religious demands of the social fractions in conflict.[94] This tends to cause the religious field to effectuate a religious production in *structural correspondence* with the social relationships of dominance present in the lay public.[95]

In this manner as well, the interests of the different social fractions in conflict have an influence—a *mediate* influence—on the *transactional religious production* (the dynamics) of the religious area.

Chapter Twenty-Three

DEMAND, PRODUCTION, AND CONSUMPTION OF RELIGIOUS GOODS

We have already observed, in Chapter Twenty-One, that religious interest in class societies with specialized religious work undergoes a conflictive and asymmetric fragmentation. At the level of the laity, it becomes a set of *religious demands* directed toward the elements that specialize in this religious work.

Then, in Chapter Twenty-Two, we indicated that it is *through* these socially diversified religious demands that the social structure acts *(mediately)* upon religious production. This production is always transactional—that is, it achieves satisfaction of the different religious demands (in exchange for recognition of the legitimacy of the religious producers) only incompletely and unequally.

In view of all this, let us focus more closely on the relationships obtaining between the religious area and social conflicts on the specifically religious level. We distinguish for this purpose three moments in the production of religious goods: the moment of *demand,* the moment of *production* properly so-called, and the moment of the *consumption* of religious goods.

1. The Religious Demand of the Laity

This demand is regulated directly by the social structure—not exclusively, it is true, but nevertheless primarily. Each social fraction, in accordance with its origin, trajectory, position, relative conjuncture, and strategy, will be found in a particular social relationship vis-à-vis the religious field in its society. In this *relationship* and this *situation*, each social fraction—again, in accordance with its origin, trajectory, position, conjuncture, and strategy—will develop its own specific set of *religious demands*, partially different from and in conflict with the religious demands of other social fractions.

The religious demands of one given social fraction do not produce, of and by themselves, religious goods (discourse, ritual, norms, objects, space, organizations, and so on) adequate for the satisfaction of this social fraction.

The religious demands of any social fraction can have an influence on religious production if, and only if, (1) they succeed in finding a differentiated institutional element—for instance, a clergy group—that will receive these demands directly and transmit them to the interior of the religious field, rendering them present there in an audible and insistent manner. And (2) they must succeed in converging with an institutional interest in the religious field—an internal opening, exigency, or weakness—that offers those demands room and space.

It is possible that one or both of these preconditions for the influence of demand on production will be lacking. In that case the demands will remain, at least provisionally, *unsatisfied*.

2. Religious Production

Religious production properly so-called is directly regulated by the internal structure of the religious field—not exclusively, it is true, but nevertheless predominantly. Each category of clergy, in accordance with its origin, trajectory, position, conjuncture, and strategy within the religious area will be found in a particular institutional situation. This situation will determine its particular dissatisfactions, attitudes, expectations, and tendencies. Each category of clergy—again, in accordance with the same parameters—will be found to be in a particular institutional relationship with the rest of the categories of clergy constituting the religious area.

Within this institutional *relationship* and this *situation*, each category of clergy, according to the parameters mentioned, will have its own set of limitations, tendencies, and possibilities with respect to *religious production*.

This set of elements will be partially different from and in asymmetric conflict with that of each of the other categories of clergy present. It will be these same limitations, tendencies, and possibilities of religious production of each category of clergy that will determine, according to the relationships of institutional power characterizing each concrete religious conjuncture, which religious goods will be produced and which will not, in what form and quantity, and how, when, where, and to whom they will be offered, distributed, and exchanged once they are produced.

As a result, the religious production of the clergy can be totally foreign to the religious demands of the laity. Nevertheless, it is practically impossible that over a prolonged period all production in the religious field would be totally foreign to any and all religious demands issuing from the laity. What *is* possible and usual, on the contrary, is that *part* of the religious production of the clergy estranges itself from lay demands. Instead it responds exclusively to intrainstitutional interests—interests arising solely out of the internal dynamics of the religious area (for example, a great part of the theological production concerning celibacy within Catholicism).

On the other hand, religious production (and the activity of the clergy in general) cannot *create* lay religious demand. The effect of religious production on the religious demands of the laity is limited in principle to its (partial and unequal) satisfaction or to its complete nonsatisfaction. Of course, the satisfaction (and its degree) of the religious demand of a social fraction by a corresponding production on the part of the clergy will condition the orientation and development of further religious demands by that social fraction. This is true especially if the original demand has its origin in a particular experience undergone by that fraction over a long period of time.

All this means that the activity of religious production by the clergy with respect to the religious demand of the laity is an *indirect* action—of satisfaction or nonsatisfaction, for the moment—and of orientation and development of this same demand for the long term.

3. Lay Religious Consumption

Lay religious consumption is directly regulated by the convergence of religious demand and supply, and indirectly by the social structure (which determines the demand) and by the structure of the religious area (which determines the supply). Each social fraction will "consume" determinate religious goods if, and only if, such goods appear *adequate* to satisfy, partially or totally, this same social fraction's own specific demands. These demands antedate religious production and are directly regulated by the social fraction's social situation and its social relationship with the corresponding religious field.

But, as is obvious, a social fraction will "consume" religious goods adequate to its demand if, and only if, such religious goods have actually been *produced* and placed at its disposal. Clearly, it is impossible to consume what has not yet been produced. In this sense, production has a direct effect on consumption—providing, or not providing, religious goods adequate to preexistent demand.

But of what is produced, only that portion is consumed that is available and adequate to preexistent demand. In this sense, religious demand (and through it, the social structure) has a direct effect on religious consumption, selecting, among the goods produced and supplied by the religious field, those that appear likely to satisfy the particular religious demand of the corresponding social fraction. And so, those religious goods will not be consumed that are either inadequate to the religious demand of the corresponding social fraction, or, although available and potentially adequate to such demand, are found to be outside the reach of the corresponding social fraction.

Briefly, neither religious demand nor religious production is capable, each by itself alone, of bringing about religious consumption. Consumption is the sole and exclusive result of the convergence of an unsatisfied religious demand with the supply of a product adequate to this demand. When, and only when, these two conditions are present, religious consumption will take place.

Religious consumption acts directly on *subsequent religious demand*. To the extent the religious demand of a given social fraction meets with an adequate production, a religious consumption will be produced that will satisfy (most often partially, and always *provisionally*) the corresponding demand. And it is the relative degree, and the duration, of this satisfaction that will determine whether the demand in question continues the same, increases, or, instead (provisionally) disappears.

By contrast, the effect of religious consumption on *subsequent religious production* is indirect. If this consumption renders the corresponding religious production *successful* (that is, a production that succeeds in branching out, finding acceptance, permeating minds and organizations, and modifying, significantly and over a long period, the behavior of the consumer social fraction—all this in accordance with the expectations and interests of religious producers), then this success will strengthen the institutional position of the producing category of clergy. It will also tend to orientate the religious field toward the pursuit of like production, thus tightening the bonds between this category and this fraction.

Contrariwise, if a lack of consumption renders the corresponding religious production *unsuccessful* (that is, having effects contrary to the expectations and interests of the religious producers), this failure will weaken the institutional position of the producing category of clergy. And it will weaken its bonds with the demanding social fraction and the corresponding religious production, thus influencing the religious area by restraining or modifying that production.[96]

As we see, the relationships among religious demand, production, and consumption are, without any doubt, multiple and complex. But they are also extraordinarily significant for understanding the dynamics of any religion within a class society with specialized religious functions.

Chapter Twenty-Four

INTERNAL STRUCTURING
OF RELIGIOUS POWER

Like all other power, *religious power* is a *capability*—at the disposition of some groups but at least provisionally denied to others. In the material under consideration, religious power will consist in the capability of producing, reproducing, storing, distributing, and exchanging religious goods.

Such a capability can be at the disposition of some groups—and denied to others—only to the extent that the former dispose of the necessary *means* of effectuating and controlling the production, reproduction, storage, distribution, and exchange of the goods in question—in this case, the means of religious production. (At least in principle, the capability of processing religious goods is determined by those who possess the means of religious *production*.) In this sense, religious power consists in proprietorship of the means of religious production.

The religious field is, precisely, that sector of society, that portion of social space, that contains, organizes, and distributes religious power. As such, the religious field is the terrain on which religious power is condensed and concentrated in its quality as *result* of preceding struggles and transactions between clergy and laity. It is the terrain on which religious power appears in its quality as *moment* of expropriation/appropriation of the means of religious production. And it is the terrain on which the struggle is waged for religious power in its quality as *object* of conflicts between clergy and laity on the one hand and, especially, among different categories of clergy on the other.

From the viewpoint of religious power, we can define "church" as that structured set of religious agents and institutions that, at a determinate moment, and in the religious field of a particular society, has acquired a *monopoly of the legitimate exercise of religious power*. A *church*, then (as defined in this specifically sociological sense), is the religious system in possession of the ability to define a religious agent or a religious action as legitimate, as well as the correlative ability to disqualify it as illegitimate. A church—in the sense defined—therefore has the ability (relative and provisional, but real and lasting) to confer *religious legitimacy* upon an agent, a teaching, an activity, or an organization. And it has the ability to deny or withdraw this same legitimacy.

Religious legitimacy is basically an expression of the state of relationships of religious force at a determinate moment in the struggle for religious power. As such, it is the result of previous struggles for the monopoly of the legitimate exercise of religious power.

The strategy that imposes itself upon a church, in its capacity as religious system monopolizing the legitimate exercise of religious power, has specific traits. These traits are sociologically meaningful, and need to be pointed out. But first may we be allowed to repeat that an *ecclesiastical strategy* is not the result of the conscious intentions of the agents constituting a church. It is the result of an inherent tendency of the *objective* position of monopoly that any church occupies in the structure of the religious field. That is, it is the result of a tendency inherent in the relationships of religious power.

The specific traits that define the strategy of a church—and differentiate it from any other type of system in the religious field—can be defined as the tendency and ability to (1) preserve the acquired monopoly of the legitimate exercise of religious power, (2) preserve and extend its own audience or public (linked to it through the mediation of relationships of demand, production, and consumption of religious goods), (3) protect itself from conflicts, crises, and sudden and repeated transformations, and (4) reproduce the basic structure of the religious field, in respect of its own set of relationships, through the maintenance of the established religious order.

The ecclesiastical strategy inherent in a church's monopolistic position can be summed up as a strategy of *reproduction of the structure of (established) religious power.*

This ecclesiastical strategy of reproduction limits and orientates the whole activity of a church, determining the basic tendencies of its own specific religious production. That is to say, religious production developed within a church, serving as it does the religious demands of the corresponding public, tends to the reproduction of the prevailing structure of religious power.

Indeed, the ecclesiastical strategy of reproduction leads every church to subordinate satisfaction of the religious demands of its own public to its interest to reproduce itself as the possessor of religious power. And this holds true even to the point where, in cases of nonnegotiable conflict between the demands of the public and its own maintenance in religious power, every church will tend to leave the demands of the public unsatisfied in favor of the maintenance of the established religious order.

Ecclesiastical strategy, in this definition, will tend to lead any and every church to institutionalize mechanisms of self-perpetuation capable of *preserving its unity and continuity,* in the midst of, and in spite of, any divisions and transformations that may be operating in the social structure or in the religious field itself.

These mechanisms—organizational and doctrinal—of the self-perpetuation of a church range from means of binding individuals to the church from infancy (baptism, confirmation, catechism, first communion, and so on, in the case of the Catholic Church), to means of specific response to social processes whose origin is extraecclesiastical but which directly or indirectly affect the life and lot of the church and its public.

They include, for example, means for creating *conjunctural organizations* to respond to governmental initiatives facilitating divorce or encouraging birth control, and the like. They include means of preventing geographical separations *(centralization),* doctrinal schisms (theological *uniformity*), and broad-based support of heresies (*closeness* of clergy and laity, recruitment of clergy among the masses, and the like).

The long, complex, and rich history of the Catholic Church offers, up to a certain point, the ideal paradigm of ecclesiastical strategy to ensure unity and continuity.[97] The specific history of Latin American Catholicism abounds in examples of such strategy.

Chapter Twenty-Five

PROPHETS AND INNOVATIONS
IN THE STRUGGLE FOR
RELIGIOUS POWER

In class societies with a specialization of religious work, the structure of the religious field is conflictive and asymmetric. The sacerdotal body in possession of a monopoly of the legitimate exercise of religious power in such a structure (that is, what we have called a "church" in the sociological sense) occupies the dominant position within this asymmetric structure.

As sociologist Pierre Bourdieu has maintained, following Max Weber, every church is in permanent danger of the rise of *prophets*—that is, of religious agents involved in a strategy of conquest of religious power, and capable of mobilizing significant sectors of the church's public against the monopoly of religious power exercised by that church.

To the extent that the religious demands of the different social fractions that make up the laity are satisfied only incompletely and unequally; to the extent that these fractions of the laity have socio-political and, correlatively, religious interests, in counterposition to one another; and to the extent that the laity has tendencies toward religious autonomy—that is, toward the reappropriation of the means of religious production expropriated by the clergy—to this triple extent there are always, in a class society with specialized religious work, the *objective social conditions* for the propulsion and support of a movement of subversion of the established religious order.

On the other hand, to the extent that the internal structure of the religious area is conflictive and asymmetric (with relationships of competition and dominance among the religious specialists); to the extent that certain categories of clergy do not find total satisfaction of their interests in each concrete conjuncture of the relationships of religious force; and to the extent that certain categories of clergy (by their origin, trajectory, position, conjuncture, or strategy) are inclined to serve as the vehicle of unsatisfied religious demands of subordinate social fractions seeking to gain their religious autonomy—to this triple extent there are always, in a class society with specialized religious work, the *objective religious conditions* for the generation and maintenance of a movement of subversion of the established religious order.

Genesis of a Prophetic Movement

Nevertheless the existence of these objective socio-religious conditions does not suffice to produce a *prophetic movement*—a growing mobilization of forces, among clergy as well as laity, explicitly calling into question the ruling mode of religious production and orientated to the curtailment of the monopoly of religious power exercised by the established sacerdotal body. In order for a prophetic movement to be launched, it is necessary for a *prophet* to arise—a person or group capable of uniting and articulating, in their words and deeds, those conditions, *social* as well as religious, that make possible (but not inevitable) the rise of such a prophetic movement.

The prophet is the person (or group) capable of rendering explicit what is implicit, of uniting what is disunited, and of formulating, in words and deeds, a set of unsatisfied religious demands. The subjects, lay and clerical, of the unsatisfied demands find their demands expressed in this prophetic formulation. They can mobilize their energies around the prophet's words and deeds.[98]

But a prophet may or may not arise. If one does not arise, then the social and religious conditions permitting the appearance of a prophetic movement will continue latent, implicit, tacit. But they encompass a potentiality for promoting a growing secret dissatisfaction, coupled with individual defections, which can still provoke a crisis of established religious power in the long run. Hence these conditions can render still more probable the appearance of a prophet and a prophetic movement.

A prophet makes innovations—discursive, ritual, organizational—in the religious field. But not every *religious innovation*[99] is a prophetic innovation. By religious innovation we understand any teaching, rite, or organization produced within the religious field that, instead of being a mere repetition of tradition, is a modification of religious goods traditionally produced in that field.

A religious innovation can be merely *adaptive*—tending to preserve the established religious order in the midst of transformations external or internal to the religious field. In this case, generally speaking, the innovation is produced and controlled by the central organs of ecclesiastical power. But a religious innovation can be genuinely *prophetic*—tending to subvert the established religious order and achieve transformations in the religious area. In this case, generally speaking, the innovation is produced on the periphery of ecclesiastical power.

In order for a prophetic movement to arise, it is necessary, as we have said, that a prophet arise within the religious field. A prophet, in the sociological sense being applied here, is a person or group capable of producing a *prophetic innovation*—that is, a religious innovation adequate to express a set of religious demands thus far unsatisfied, and capable of mobilizing around itself a growing assemblage of forces, lay and clerical, set to transform the prevailing structure of the religious area. It is prophetic innovation that typifies a prophet as such, and, in this sense, constitutes the essence of any prophetic movement.[100]

Every prophetic movement—inasmuch as it constitutes an objective threat to the monopoly of legitimate exercise of religious power on the part of a church—provokes reactions against itself on the part of ecclesiastical power. These antiprophetic reactions of ecclesiastical power tend to *exclude* the most refractory representatives of the prophetic movement,[101] *recover* the most vacillating followers of the movement, *partially disqualify* the prophetic innovation of which this movement is the vessel and subject, and *partially incorporate* the same innovation in order to set up an obstacle to its control by the prophetic movement and to satisfy in part the demands that have permitted its appearance.

The probability of success of a prophet, a prophetic innovation, or a prophetic movement varies with (1) the relationships of extrareligious force, and the type of bond established between these relationships and the prophetic movement, and (2) the relationships of intrareligious force and the properly religious characteristics of the prophetic innovation.

1. Extrareligious Factors

In a time of general crisis for a whole society, especially at moments in which social movements spring up,[102] the probability of the appearance of prophetic movements in the religious field increases. In these circumstances, to the extent the prophetic movement is linked to a social movement and receives support from it, its chances of success increase.[103]

As Bourdieu has also pointed out, the success of a prophet is incomprehensible from a purely intrareligious analysis. One must transcend the framework of the religious field and analyze the extrareligious social forces present, and their relationship with the religious forces in competition with one another, in order to explain the success, as also the failure, of a prophet.

2. Intrareligious Factors

There are properly religious traits that may facilitate or impede the success of a prophetic innovation. If the *factors of legitimation of the innovation* are internal to the church itself, the probability of the exclusion of the prophet and the prophet's followers are less than when the sources of legitimation are external to the church.[104]

If the prophetic innovation is somehow within the purview of ecclesiastical restriction to *fidelity to tradition* (never denying anything officially asserted in the past), the probability of its official disqualification will be less than in the case where such innovation represents a total break with ecclesiastical tradition. If the innovation's doctrinal content does not transcend the limits of a *commentary on the foundational proclamation* of the church—that is, if it keeps within the limits of an interpretation of the foundational message—the probability of its success will be greater.

Finally, it must be kept in account that the *socio-historical trajectory* traversed by any church defines certain limits of tolerance. Its rigidity will be in proportion to the importance of this church's linkage with (and the length of time this church has existed in) a determinate social system. If a prophetic innovation is so closely linked to a social strategy foreign to the church in question that it transgresses these limits of tolerance, it will almost irreversibly provoke its own exclusion.[105]

Chapter Twenty-Six

FORCES SHAPING THE SOCIOLOGICAL REALITY OF A RELIGIOUS INSTITUTION

Mutations in the religious field, more particularly those of religious systems and institutions, are not, in spite of the impression that may have been gathered in a rapid reading of Part II, merely the product of social structures and conflicts. No, social structures and conflicts make *possible* certain mutations in the religious field (and in the systems and institutions of this field). In fact, social structures and conflicts limit and orientate, in various ways, transformations in the religious field.

Once rendered socially possible, mutations of the religious field become *real* only to the extent (1) that there is *an innovative production* (whether adaptive or prophetic) *in the religious field*, and (2) that there are *objective conditions within that same religious field permitting the relative success of such innovative production*.

If there is no innovative production within the religious field, the vitality of the religion in question will be reduced either to its own simple reproduction, or to a slow decadence of the religious system. This will happen even in the case where significant transformations occur in the corresponding social structure. It will happen even where there is a religious innovation (adaptive or prophetic), but internal conditions of the religious field impede its development.

A religion, any religion, is a specific reality, with a consistency of its own, one whose particularities define an internal complexus of *limits, possibilities, and orientations*. That is, its particularities will define, in a given stage of its development, what will be impossible for it, what will be possible, and what it will actually tend to bring about within the realm of the possible. In other words, the specifics of each religion determine the spectrum of possibilities for its activities and innovations. They determine as well which of these activities and innovations are the most likely to be undertaken by the agents of that religion.

A religion has a *history* and a *tradition*, a *teaching* and an *organization*, a

110

position in the religious field and an internal social *composition*, a *public*, and *resources*. Each one of these elements acts as a particular social *force*, drawing, in a manner that is *variable* with each concrete case, that religion in a specific *direction* and with a specific *intensity*.

Its *history*—the history of each particular religion—implants in its agents a whole series of habits, rhythms, and expectations that hold it to a certain *continuity* with the past. This renders impossible or difficult certain transformations that, according to the magnitude of the internal or external forces ready to accomplish them, would imply a breach with the past—a breach that would bring this religion to a situation of crisis and disorientation.

The *tradition* of every religion leads it in the direction of a certain *reiteration* of what has in the past been officially maintained within it. In proportion to the degree to which its ambient threatens a traditional posture, tradition comes up with prohibitions of and obstacles to the defense of positions condemned in the past, or condemnations of positions defended in the past. Otherwise the credibility of the religion could be considered to be in jeopardy.

Its *teachings*, especially the foundational teaching of this same religion, constitute a warning to it not to transgress the limits fixed by its doctrinal structure and content. It obliges it to develop, in each new situation, a *reinterpretation* of this same doctrine. Failure to do so can open the door to a reappropriation of the foundational teaching by groups capable of carrying into effect a schismatic strategy within the religious system in question.

Its *organization*—of agents and institutions—constrains it to *reproduce* the same organization. It erects obstacles to any initiative involving profound organizational transformation, even when there are marked tendencies in this direction, for fear of disorganization and defections that might result from such a transformation.[106]

Its *position*—in the overall structure of the religious field—impels it to a strategy of *preservation* of acquired religious power as a minimum, and expansion as a maximum. It erects barriers to any innovation that could place this acquired power in danger, even in the presence of other forces tending to introduce the innovation.

Its internal social *composition*—the configuration of functionaries who administer the religion—obliges it to the *satisfaction* of the heterogeneous exigencies of the competing categories of clergy within it, under pain of fostering the development of conflicts and breaches that would threaten its unity and continuity.

Its *public*—the mass of laity who sustain and legitimize the social existence of the religion—pressures it to submit to a certain *adaptation* to the (multiple, variable, conflictive, and asymmetric) religious demands arising with each transformation of the social conditions of each social fraction present. Otherwise it runs the risk of debilitation through abandonment and opposition on the part of significant groups of laity.

Finally, the religion's *resources* force it to a certain *rationalization* of their use, closing off the possibility of certain activities for whose realization it lacks the appropriate means, and permitting others that are feasible within the framework of its available resources. It also orientates the religion toward a use of the resources that will guarantee the preservation of the accustomed sources of supply of these resources (even stimulating their development, if possible).

Any religion, then, must maintain continuity with its history. It must maintain its tradition, respect the limits of its foundational doctrine, reproduce its organization, guard its power, satisfy the exigencies of its functionaries, adapt to the demands of its heterogeneous public, and use its resources in a rational manner. The reality of a determinate religion in a specific context is the geometrical *result* of the polygon of these forces, and perhaps others as well, drawing this religion in different directions and with various degrees of traction.

In certain historico-social circumstances, this result may be the self-perpetuation, simple or extended, of the religious system, or its adaptation or reform. In other circumstances, on the contrary, the result may be the regression, asphyxiation, decadence, dismemberment, or division of the religion concerned. In either case, it is only by keeping account of the complexity of the facts of reality that we shall be able to grasp how far a determinate religion's possibilities can take it in the direction of self-reformation, and why they take it only this far—independently of the desires and intentions of the religious agents.

PART IV

Religion as an Active Factor in Social Conflicts

The course of the exposition of our theoretical framework has now traversed its first two stages: that of the analysis of the religious field as *product* of social conflicts, and that of its analysis as relatively autonomous *terrain* of social conflicts. But, with all that we have said, it must already be clear that the religious field is neither simply and solely a product of social conflicts, nor an absolutely independent reality without any connection with social conflicts.

The religious area is a reality that is both *partially produced* by social relationships (including, for our purposes, conflictive relationships among social classes), and *partially autonomous* (that is, having its own specific activity). Nevertheless, relationships between the religious field and social conflicts go beyond these two aspects that we have already analyzed. The religious field undergoes the influence of social conflicts, and develops its own conflictive dynamics. But to stop here—to rest content with what we have seen in Parts II and III—would be tantamount to asserting that religion has no significant influence upon social conflicts, upon the very structuring and development of these conflicts themselves.

In other words, were we to leave our theoretical framework at the point at which it has now arrived, it would appear that society acts on religion, and that religion acts on itself, but not that religion acts on society and social conflicts. There would still be lacking (at the very least) a third aspect of the relationships between social conflicts and the religious area—the influence of the religious area on social conflicts.

Indeed, from our sociological point of view, this is the aspect in which we are most basically interested: that of the *religious conditioning of social struggles*—or, to use a more traditional sociological language, that of the "social functions of religion."

Part IV will concentrate specifically on this aspect of religion—that of the effects, the influence, of the religious field upon social conflicts. We shall be seeing the religious field as *producer* of social relationships—especially as producer of conflictive relationships among social classes. And once more, we shall situate this new dimension within the specific Latin American reality of the present day.[107]

Chapter Twenty-Seven

RELIGION AS A MEANS OF THE ACTIVITY OF SOCIETY UPON ITSELF

Human beings—whether they know it or not—produce their social relationships, their own social configuration or organization, their forms of collective structuring. They produce their society.[108] But they do not produce it directly, immediately, and mechanically. No, human beings produce their social relationships through actions limited and orientated by (among other things) a shared *worldview*.[109]

The worldview any social group adopts, based on its long and complex collective experience, permits it, as we saw in Part III, to situate and orientate itself, and to act, in its natural and social milieu. By "permit" we mean make it *possible* to situate and orientate itself, and to act. But any worldview, at the same time as it *opens up* certain possibilities, *excludes* others, and *leads* the group that is the subject of this worldview toward the possibilities it has opened up.

Any worldview, when it opens up determinate possibilities for activity, also limits and orientates the very activity it enables. Without a worldview, no human group can produce, reproduce, or transform its social relationships; but every determinate worldview limits and orientates the possibilities of the production, reproduction, and transformation of social relationships that it has made possible.

Thus the worldview of any society or social group, simultaneous with being (partially) a product of the social relationships characterizing the group or society, becomes a reality that renders possible, limits, and orientates the production, reproduction, and transformation of the same social relationships within which it has arisen. To this same extent, the worldview developed by a society or social group, from a point of departure in certain of its social relationships, plays an active role in the further development of these same social relationships. It influences them, it conditions them.

One of the basic aspects of every religion is its function in shaping a determinate worldview. The common interest entertained by all human beings,

115

social groups, and communities to have a worldview that will permit them to situate and orientate themselves, and to act, in the most satisfactory manner possible in their socio-natural milieu becomes, for some societies and social groups, a properly religious interest. That is, it becomes an interest in having a worldview with a clear reference to the supernatural and metasocial forces upon which these groups and societies feel themselves dependent, and before which they consider themselves obliged to a certain behavior in community.

In such societies and social groups—in such subjects of religious interest—religion functions as the *terrain of mediation* of their activity upon themselves and upon their socio-natural surroundings. In such societies and social groups, human beings—whether they know it or not—produce, reproduce, and transform their social relationships by activities that are rendered possible, limited, and orientated by their religious worldview—their religion.

Intellectual work in general, and religious work in its intellectual component, consists in the *transformation of the socially lived into the socially thought.*[110] In other words, it consists in the subjective structuration of objective collective experience. Every religion, inasmuch as it transforms the socially lived into the socially thought (and thought with reference to supernatural and metasocial forces), reconstructs subjectively the objective experience of the social groups of believers in a particular manner. In so doing, religion establishes the lines of demarcation, the inclusions and exclusions, the associations and the oppositions, that will render possible the communicable organization of a collectivity's past experience.

Thus each religion—as a work of transformation of the socially lived into the socially thought—will define, for certain social groups, the thinkable and the unthinkable, the desirable and the undesirable, the possible and the impossible, the useful and the harmful, the important and the secondary, the urgent and the nonurgent, the forbidden, the permitted, and the obligatory, the obvious and the dubious, the absolute and the relative.[111]

In the course of effecting this structuration of collective experience, every religion makes it possible for its adherents to act upon their socio-natural surroundings. It offers them an understandable and communicable representation of those surroundings, which is a *conditio sine qua non* of all human activity, individual or collective. And in making this activity possible, every religious worldview limits and orientates the further activity of this group of believers.

A religion can have an influence upon the development of society—can fulfill social functions—precisely because, in the first place, every religion *limits and orientates the behavior of the believing groups* within it. It offers them an understandable and communicable representation of the world. At the same time that this representation organizes the experience lived by this group, it situates and guides it in its socio-natural surroundings.

Every religion, inasmuch as it organizes in a comprehensible and communicable manner (that is, as it gives meaning to) the collective experience of a social group, thereby constitutes a fundamental element (and in some cases the very nucleus) of the believing group's *consciousness* and *identity*. Believers *know* the world—perceive it and think it—*through* their religious worldview. By that very fact their activity upon that world is guided and directed by this perception of the world that their religion makes possible, limits, and orientates.

Likewise, believers *know* themselves—perceive and think themselves—*through* their religious view of the world (of which they form the center). They are held together and identified in their activity by this perception of themselves made possible, limited, and orientated by their religion. This is why a religion can have an influence on the development of a society—why it can fulfill social functions.

In class societies with specialization of religious work, the production of a religious worldview for the satisfaction of the religious interest of certain social groups (or all the members of the society) is an activity carried on by a body of functionaries specifically charged with this task. In such societies, the field formed by the interrelationships of these functionaries and the institutions in which they are organized—the religious field—constitutes the element, or one of the elements, with the social assignment of effecting the transformation of the socially lived into the socially thinkable and communicable. In this sense, in such societies the religious field is the element (or at least one element) with the social assignment of reconstructing, in a communicable and satisfactory manner, the collective experience of the subjects of the corresponding religious interest.

In view of what we have stated, we can maintain that the religious area is a medium of activity in which society acts upon itself. In order for human beings to produce, reproduce, and transform their relationships—that is, in order for society to act upon itself—it is necessary that they perceive their socio-natural surroundings in a comprehensible and communicable manner. This necessitates a comprehensible and communicable representation of collective experience in the form of a worldview, shared by the collectivity in question, that will permit these human beings to situate and orientate themselves, and therefore be able to act upon, their socio-natural surroundings.

Because, in class societies with specialization in religious work, the religious field is a social element whose function it is to develop a worldview such as that described, the religious field will therefore carry out a work of *mediation* of society's activity upon itself. It will render thinkable the collectivity's experience, in order to render possible the continuation of that experience.[112]

Chapter Twenty-Eight

SOCIAL FUNCTIONS OF RELIGION: SOCIOLOGICAL VARIABLES

To the extent that religious production consists in a work of mediation of society's activity upon itself, to this same extent a religion will be able to have an influence on the production, reproduction, and transformation of social relationships. That is, it will be able to perform social functions.

Functionalist Theory of Religion

In the history of the sociology of religions, the social functions of religion have been studied under the marked influence of the functionalist school.[113] According to this socio-anthropological school of thought (whose analyses are for the most part interesting and fertile), religion *always fulfills the same social functions*: psychological security, social cohesion, a sacralization of the social structure, and so on. These functions, it is maintained, converge with others toward the maintenance of the internal harmonious equilibrium of a society.

For functionalism, every religion, in whatever social context it may be located, and in each of the phases of development of that context, tends always—solely and exclusively—to fulfill the same functions. That is, for functionalism, religion tends always to function in support of the maintenance of the internal harmonious equilibrium of a society. And just as, for this school, social conflict is a transitory and, as it were, accidental reality in the functioning of society, so the absence of a contribution by religion to the social equilibrium will be seen by this current of thought as an equally accidental and transitory *dysfunction*. That is, any "dysfunction" on the part of religion amounting to a noncontribution to the social equilibrium in a given social context will be perceived as something anomalous, sociopathic.

This is not the place for an in-depth critique of the functionalist theory of religion.[114] But I want to point out what radically separates my own theoretical option from that of the functionalists. For those of us who do not subscribe to functionalism,[115] the sociological analysis of religion must free itself of the altogether indemonstrable functionalist prejudice that religion is a set

118

of fixed social functions, present in every society, and that all religion, in any society, always performs only these same functions.

Instead, we endorse a hypothesis that, it seems to us, is much more fertile, to say the least. We hold (1) that the social functions of a religion can vary with the history, structure, and articulation of each particular society and religious system. And we hold (2) that the only scientifically valid way to establish the *particular* social functions of a particular religion, in a concrete, determinate social context, is on the basis of an empirical examination of the pertinent social and socio-religious phenomena.

In other words, to us "*the* social function of religion in general in society in general" is meaningless. It is all the more meaningless because it is held that this function can be established *a priori*, antecedent to any examination of a concrete set of social and socio-religious phenomena. After all, we are treating of the particular social functions of a particular religious system in a particular society, situated in space and time. This is something that can be established only *a posteriori*—after an empirical investigation of the phenomena we want to analyze.

Social Variables

We have already stated, based on reasons set forth in the preceding chapter, that religions can perform certain social functions. That is, they can condition and influence the production, reproduction, and transformation of social relationships. Now we add that the social functions that a religion can perform in a determinate social context—the ways in which a religion can condition and influence the development of certain social relationships—are *variables*.

The functions performed by Catholicism today in Chile can be different from, and even opposed to, the functions performed by this same Catholic Church today in Venezuela. The functions performed by the Catholic Church today in Chile can be different from (and even incompatible with) the functions performed by this same church in Chile half a century ago. The functions performed by Catholicism today in Chile can be different from (and even contrary to) the functions performed there today by the Church of Jesus Christ of Latter-Day Saints, the Mormons. In fact, the functions performed today by the Catholic Church in Chile in regard to the Chilean working class through the *JOC* (*Juventud Obrera Católica*, Young Catholic Workers) can be radically contrary to those performed today by this church in regard to the Chilean business community through Opus Dei. Indeed, as far as we can learn from observation and reports coming out of Chile, the data suggest precisely this hypothesis.

When we say that the functions of a religion in a determinate social context are *variable*, we mean that such functions can vary—even to the point that the same religion, in the same context, can perform contradictory and conflictive functions.

It should not be necessary to note that the social functions of any religion, in any context, depend very little, if at all, upon the consciousness and intentions of the religious agents there involved. Such functions depend especially on objective conditions in the society in question—on the situation of the religious field in this society and the internal circumstances of the religious area itself.

Accordingly, the social functions of a religion in a determinate social context can vary according to historical, structural, and conjunctural variations in the religious field. They can vary from one time to another, from one place to another, from one social group to another, from one religion to another, and from one category of clergy to another.

Thus it is that, in a class society with religious specialization, the same religious system can fulfill various functions—complementary or contradictory—with regard to each of the different social classes. And with respect to the same class, the social functions of the same religious system can vary from one phase to another of the development of this class or this religious system.

Then too, the importance of the functions, the degree of influence, and the level of conditioning exercised by "religion" on "society" (because they are always exercised by *this* religion on *this* society) are also *variable* relationships. In certain circumstances a statement issued by the Catholic Church can unleash a civil war or a coup d'etat. The same discourse, produced in the same country and by the same church but in other circumstances, can occupy a minuscule space in two or three newspapers and have no further consequences. A call by the bishops to "stop the strike" can, under certain circumstances, occasion a massive return of laborers to the factories and the provisional renunciation by these laborers of the demands that motivated the strike. In other circumstances a similar episcopal call can be ignored, or even provoke a reaction in the form of union protest against interference by the church in "nonreligious matters."

The importance of a religion in a society, like its social functions, is variable. It can change, according to the historical, structural, and conjunctural mutations of either the society or the religious field. The same religion can have a different degree of influence, according to the time, place, and social group in which it functions.[116]

Nevertheless, the tendency of any religion is to effect a certain *totalization* of individual and collective experience. That is, any religion tends to organize all experience—past, present, and future—of persons as well as groups, in reference to supernatural and metasocial forces. This tendency has the effect, in those groups and communities in which religion plays a certain role, of endowing religion with a decisive influence in the conditioning of collective behavior.

In our own perspective—that of a critico-political sociology of religions in Latin America—what particularly interests us is the functions that the religious area can perform with regard to social conflicts. We are interested in analyzing the religious field as one of the social terrains of *mediation*, or production, of social conflicts. Hence we shall be concerned, throughout the remainder of Part IV, with a study of the religious field as a locus of obstacles to, and aids for, the struggle of the dominant classes to achieve and consolidate their *hegemony*, and of the antagonistic struggle of some dominated classes to achieve and consolidate their *autonomy*.

First we shall attempt a theoretical reconstruction of the conditions and modalities in which the religious field can function as an obstacle to the autonomy of the subordinate classes, and as an instrument of the hegemony of the dominant classes. Then, in the final chapters, we shall attempt a theoretical reconstruction of the conditions and modalities in which, on the contrary, the religious field can function to prevent the hegemony of dominant classes, and, correlatively, as a medium for the autonomy of subordinate classes.

Chapter Twenty-Nine

INCORPORATION OF RELIGION INTO THE HEGEMONIC STRATEGY OF DOMINANT CLASSES

In Chapter Sixteen ("Religion in the Dynamics of Class Dominance"), we saw that dominant classes have an *interest* and *material means* of placing religions at the service of the expansion, deepening, and consolidation of their dominance. We pointed out that the dynamics of dominance tends toward the attainment of the *hegemony* of the dominant classes—that is, toward the achievement of general acceptance of that dominance on the part of all individuals and groups of the society in question. We emphasized that this *hegemonic strategy* of the dominant classes imposed an important set of limitations and orientations on religious activity in any class society. They are limitations and orientations directed toward making the religion of that society an instrument in the service of the hegemonic strategy of the dominant classes.

Throughout Chapter Sixteen, we were looking at the relationship between hegemony and religion from one angle only. We were observing how the hegemonic strategy of any dominant class limits and orientates the religious activity carried on in a class society. We did not make explicit reference to how religions can influence society and favor the establishment of the hegemony of a bloc of dominant classes. This is what we shall do now.

Hegemonic Strategy

Let us make a first approach to our problem in terms of this question: How does the hegemonic strategy of a bloc of dominant classes limit and orientate the activities of religions with a view to having them act in favor of this hegemonic strategy?[117]

When a social class—or bloc of classes—has managed to gain a dominant position within a given society, this class (or bloc) finds itself impelled (independently of the awareness or intentions of its members in this respect) to preserve and consolidate this dominant position, along with the advantages and privileges inherent in it.

All the mechanisms of this class (or bloc) are therefore placed at the service of this interest. To this end, the greatest possible support is sought for the form of organization of society that this class (or bloc) promotes—the broadest possible base of social support for the preservation and consolidation of the type of dominance characterizing this class (or bloc).

For this reason the strategy of this class (or bloc) is oriented toward an alliance with the sectors quantitatively or qualitatively more influential in the organization and development of the society in which this class (or bloc) dominates and is interested in continuing to dominate. But in parallel fashion, this strategy of preservation and consolidation of its dominant position demands a struggle on the part of this class (or bloc) against all individuals, groups, and movements directly or potentially threatening its dominant position.

The efforts of a dominant class (or bloc) will thus tend to be exerted upon the religious field of its society, especially if this religious field exerts a profound influence on the behavior of large groups of that society.

Such efforts will, on the one hand, be orientated to obtaining from the religious field the production of practices and discourses that will legitimize and sacralize this dominance, and point to it as something desired by supernatural and metasocial forces.

But on the other hand, the efforts exerted by this class (or bloc) on religious activity in its society will be directed to obtaining from the religious area the production of practices and discourses that disqualify, delegalize, desacralize, and definitely present as *not* desired by supernatural and metasocial forces, any individuals, groups, and movements directly threatening the dominant position of this same class. At the least, every dominant class will seek to obtain from the religious field that it *not* produce any practice or discourse *favorable* to the struggle of subordinate classes against the hegemony of the dominant classes.

These efforts of the dominant classes to obtain from the religious field the sacralization of their domination and the desacralization of any struggles against it, are exerted through various dimensions of social life.

Economic Strategies

At the level of the dominant classes' strictly economic strategies of extended self-perpetuation,[118] these classes seek to create links with the highest categories of clergy in their society. For example, they bestow privileges and property on them. The purpose is to incorporate the clergy into the form of economic organization of society promoted by these classes, and to create obligations, more implicit than explicit, that will generate in the clergy a feeling of indebtedness toward these same dominant classes, and to the social system in which they are dominant.

Family Strategies

At the level of the dominant classes' family strategies of extended self-perpetuation, these classes seek to create bonds of affinity with the highest categories of clergy in their society. For example, they favor church marriages, baptismal sponsorship, or the religious profession of one of their offspring. The purpose is to incorporate the clergy into the lifestyle of the dominant classes, and to create in the clergy sentiments of indebtedness to and identity with these classes.[119]

Juridico-Political Strategies

At the level of the dominant classes' juridico-political strategies of extended self-perpetuation, they tend to create legal mechanisms that will foster the development of religious tendencies favorable to their own hegemonic strategy, afford privileges to (and create bonds with) the categories of clergy closest to their own interests, and stunt the growth of religious movements opposed to their dominance. From this viewpoint, concordats, patronage agreements, and other forms of mutual church/state recognition can be interpreted as implicit (or not so implicit) transactions in which dominant classes grant juridical privileges to a religion in exchange for a control over religious activity against their hegemony.

Educational and Cultural Strategies

At the level of the dominant classes' educational and cultural strategies of extended self-perpetuation, these classes attempt to create (or strengthen) cultural processes and educational institutions favoring the propagation of ideas most in accord with their own interests. They attempt to incorporate the clergy in those processes and in the administration of those institutions so that the clergy itself will be molded in the mentality of the dominant classes. They can thus serve as conduits for the transmission (and sacralization) of the same mentality.[120]

Repressive Strategies

Finally, at the level of the dominant classes' repressive strategies of extended self-perpetuation, these classes seek, in certain cases, to impose external acceptance of religions favorable to the maintenance of the established order. And they seek to penalize any religious (or antireligious) activity directly opposed to the status quo (for example, by fines, imprisonment, exile, and so on).

If all these strategies of extended self-perpetuation of the dominant classes, each in its own sector, succeed, in a given society, in prolonging themselves through several generations, without significant failures or stagnation, the probable result will be the development of a mutual penetration, identification, and feeling of obligation and respect between clergy and dominant classes. It will be of such nature and intensity that, imperceptibly and unconsciously, the religious production of the clergy will gradually converge with the general strategy of the dominant classes. That is, religious production will structure itself more and more favorably to the hegemony of the dominant classes, and more and more unfavorably to struggles against this dominance.

Chapter Thirty

THE CLERICAL CONTRIBUTION TO THE HEGEMONIC STRATEGY OF THE DOMINANT

How can a given clergy—that is, a stable body of functionaries specifically assigned the task of religious production within a class society—contribute, independently of its awareness and its intentions, to the consolidation of the domination of a class (or bloc of classes) in the society in which this clergy acts?

In those communities and social groups that are the bearers, the subjects, of religious interest, the group's perception of its socio-natural surroundings, and hence its behavior, individual and collective, in these surroundings, are limited and orientated by its religious worldview. That is, its perception and behavior with regard to these surroundings are *structured* by its religious system—by its religion.

If the production of this religious system is monopolized by a clergy, and if this clergy has been incorporated into the hegemonic strategy of the dominant classes, religious production will tend to be carried out in such a way that this clergy's public will (1) reconstruct its experience, and hence perceive its socio-natural surroundings, in accord with the interests of the dominant classes. Consequently, this clergy's public (2) will act in a manner favorable to the hegemonic strategy of these same dominant classes.

In other words, a clergy that has been successfully subjected to the dominant classes' strategy of extended self-perpetuation will tend spontaneously and unconsciously to produce, preserve, reproduce, propagate, and inculcate religious teachings and practices in accord with the interests of these dominant classes. Likewise a clergy in mutual penetration and identification with the dominant classes, and "indebted" to them, will tend to exclude, disqualify, and desacralize any teachings and practices, religious or not, that appear to be opposed to the interests of the dominant classes.

In such circumstances, the clergy in question, even without knowing it, will generate a restructuration of the religious system in its hands. This restructuration will tend to create a *consent* to established dominance, and a simultaneous *rejection* of opposition to such dominance.

This consent and rejection, in turn, with their reference to supernatural and metasocial forces, and aroused in a public that is a bearer and subject of a refined religious interest, will have a tendency to constitute a strong bond of cohesion of the public in question with the dominant social classes.

Through what concrete channels does this clergy effect such a religious structuration of consent to dominance? A complete list of the channels and modalities of the (unconscious, indeed involuntary, hence all the more efficacious) religious structuration of social consent to dominance would be endless. Furthermore such channels and modalities will vary from one concrete context to another. Let us nevertheless attempt to delineate certain avenues of such structuration, which may serve to sharpen the focus of our general theoretical propositions.

To this purpose I shall simply list a few types of religious production that, in the specific context of official Latin American Catholicism today, seem to me to be cooperating in the hegemonic strategy of the bourgeoisie on our continent:[121]

—Production of a religious discourse couched quantitatively and qualitatively in terms that are innocuous and foreign to the basic conflicts of a class society.[122]

—Production of a religious discourse that assigns priority to struggles and conflicts that are distinct from the fundamental social conflicts of the societies in question, and tend to draw attention away from them.

—Production of a religious discourse explicitly denying the existence or importance of a social division between dominating and dominated.

—Production of a religious discourse that, although recognizing the existence, and at times even the importance, of the division between dominating and dominated, explicitly denies the legitimacy of a struggle against this social division.

—Production of a religious discourse that recognizes the legitimacy of a struggle against certain aspects of the conflict between dominating and dominated—in matters of poverty, illiteracy, and the like—but explicitly disqualifies the struggle against the existence of dominating classes.

—Production of a religious discourse that, even though it criticizes the dominating classes for certain "abuses," attributes to them alone the ability and the authority to correct the "negative aspects" of their dominance.

—Production of a religious discourse that accepts the prevailing social, economic, political, juridical, and cultural order as something beyond question.

—Production of a religious discourse explicitly soliciting the acceptance and defense of the prevailing social, economic, political, juridical, and cultural order.

—Production of a religious discourse that portrays the established order as the result of divine punishment or of the workings of divine providence.

—Production of a religious discourse that refers to those who hold power as depositories of a sacred and eternal authority, which ought to remain as it is, and consequently must be obeyed under the pain of divine punishment.

—Production of a religious discourse that portrays the dominated as persons who (by way of punishment or providence) ought submissively to accept their subordinate condition.

—Production of a religious discourse that explicitly condemns struggles of the dominated against dominators.

—Nonproduction of a religious discourse that explicitly condemns dominance and its consequences for the dominated.

—Nonproduction of a religious discourse explicitly encouraging struggle against the established order.

—The presence, showing tacit or explicit approval, of official representatives of the clergy in activities, processes, and institutions whose purpose is the expansion or commendation of the established order (the founding of private enterprises and government projects, social or political celebrations by power blocs, military chaplaincies, and so on).

—The absence of official representatives of the clergy in activities, processes, and institutions whose purpose is the expansion or commendation of struggles against the established order (unions, strikes, labor demonstrations, political parties opposed to class dominance, celebrations of popular victories, and so on).

—Production of religious discourse or activity that explicitly condemns the presence of unofficial representatives of the clergy in activities, processes, and institutions whose purpose is the expansion or commendation of struggles against the established order.

Surely this is a long enough list. Of course we could have had a longer one, with classification by category, and concrete illustrative cases. But I have sought only to point out a few modalities by which it is possible to produce religious practices and discourses that can support and consolidate the hegemonic strategy inherent in any dominant bloc and any class society.

My only concern has been to make clear by a few examples that it is possible to produce religious practices and discourses that will favor a mental reconstruction of the world in such associations, distinctions, and oppositions as will seem to place supernatural forces on the side of the dominators— in favor of their dominance and in alignment against those who struggle against this domination.

Such a religious representation of the world, if it manages to inculcate itself in the mentality of the public of the religious system concerned, will be converted into the solid basis of consent that dominators require in order to reinforce their domination, their own way of structuring and orientating social life—their *power*.

Chapter Thirty-One

TRANSFORMING RELIGIOUS STRUCTURES IN FAVOR OF A NEW HEGEMONY

It might appear, from what has been said, that I hold that the conservative function that a religious system can perform in a class society will be performed exclusively, or at least basically, through the diffusion of a religious *product* (presence or absence of discourses and practices) adequate to the interests of the dominant classes. But this is not the case. It is not only through certain religious contents that a religious system can, in favorable circumstances, perform a conservative function in class societies. Certain forms of structuring the *mode of religious production* may, under certain social circumstances, perform conservative functions.

Populations with an Undifferentiated Self-Perpetuating Religious Tradition

In the case of such a population, expropriation of its means of religious production, when the population is on the way to becoming dominated, is one of the socio-religious processes that may be included in the hegemonic strategy of the class bloc on its way to becoming dominant. For to the extent that this population becomes dispossessed of the means of producing a religious worldview suitable for orientating it in its struggle against the dominance that threatens it—and to the extent, therefore, that the producers of its new religious worldview are not members of this population—to this double extent, the possibilities increase for reducing that population to a subordinate position.

Dispossessed of its means of religious production, a population loses a means of preserving its own autonomy. With respect to the production of its own worldview, this population passes to a state of subjection under the rule of a minority.

In addition, because religious production *for* this population passes into the hands of *another* group, either external or internal to it, it therefore fails to facilitate, and generally will prevent, the religious view thus produced from expressing and genuinely strengthening the general interests of autonomy of the population concerned. After all, it is easier for a dominant class to influence a small group of religious functionaries than directly to modify the religious view of a whole population under its domination.

Societies with a Single Specialized Religious System

In the case of class societies with this type of religious system, which has had a long and deep involvement in history, and has satisfactorily served these societies as a means of orientation, expression, communication, and defense, the efforts of an alien class to dominate the whole society will necessarily be concentrated on an attempt to transform the religious system.

This transformation, by no means easy to accomplish, will tend to be directed toward the restructuring of the religious system in such a way that its functioning and production will be adequate to the hegemonic interests of the class on its way to becoming dominant. If the resistance of the threatened community can be overcome, such a transformation may be effected through the conversion of its religious functionaries to the worldview of the class on its way to becoming dominant.

In this case—as also in the case of the opposite extreme of *annihilation and replacement* of a people's traditional religious system—the strategy of the dominant classes is basically the same. It seeks to place the religious system of the dominated population under the direct or indirect control of the dominant classes, in order simultaneously to prevent the subordinate classes from gaining autonomy by the religious route, and to facilitate the task of imposing a new religious consent favorable to the hegemony of the dominant classes.

In each alternative, if the effort of the dominant classes succeeds, the religion in question will be oriented to the performance of a conservative role with respect to their dominance.

Societies with a Pluralistic Religious Field

In the case of class societies with specialized religious functions in a *plurisystemic religious field* (as Houtart calls it—that is, a pluralistic[123] religious area, containing various religious systems conflictively and asymmetrically structured), things will happen somewhat differently.

Here the hegemonic strategy of the dominant classes will have to be directed toward the conversion or neutralization (or, in extreme cases, the annihilation and replacement) of the functionaries of the religious system having the greatest number of adherents among the potentially revolutionary subordinate classes of the society in question. This will generally be the *dominant religious system* in the religious field of this society.

As a general rule, in the case of class societies with a plurisystemic religious field, a relationship of transaction is established between the new dominant classes and the traditionally dominant religious system. This transactional relationship, taking its point of departure in the pledge of reciprocal reinforcement, ends by rendering the dominant *religion* the religion of the dominant *classes*. The religion of the majority of the members of the dominant classes becomes the dominant religion. It is the most efficient vehicle of a worldview capable of procuring the consent of the subordinate classes to the dominance exercised by the dominators.

When, on the other hand, such a transaction fails—for political, religious, or other reasons—the strategy of the dominant classes then tends to be orientated toward the reinforcement of the subordinate religious movement with the greatest potentialities for (1) weakening the power of the dominant religious system, (2) drawing away massive sectors of the subordinate classes previously devoted to the traditionally dominant religion, and (3) contributing to the procurement of consent among the subordinate classes to the domination exercised by dominators.[124] In either case—whether or not the dominant bloc succeeds in establishing a transactional relationship with the dominant religious system—the strategy of the dominant classes is directed toward the elimination of subordinate religious sects that seem capable of mobilizing the subordinate classes against their domination. And here there will be a convergence of the tendencies of the dominant classes and the dominant religious systems, in any class society with a plurisystemic religious area.[125]

In each of these three cases, the imposition of a new model of social development by a bloc of classes on its way to becoming dominant demands that a certain *religious content* be produced, in order to sponsor and justify the new type of social organization. This we saw in the two preceding chapters.

Imposition of a new model of social organization generally also demands the transformation of the *relationships of religious production*—the mode of religious production. This is necessary in order for its structure to facilitate the procurement of massive religious consent to the new model of social organization, and simultaneously to impede the religious autonomy of subordinate classes.

Chapter Thirty-Two

CONSERVATIVE FUNCTIONS
OF CHURCH SYSTEMS

We understand "church" in its strictly sociological sense. And we understand it as opposed both to "sect"[126] and "religious movement."[127] "Church," then, means that type of religious system having (1) a public that is relatively stable, massive, and composed of distinct social classes—dominant as well as subordinate—of the society in which it functions; (2) a perceptible trajectory within this same society, at least several generations old; (3) a body of monotheistic beliefs and moral norms codified into a body of doctrine with a long tradition; (4) a corps of functionaries, hierarchized, stabilized, and centralized in an organization at least several generations old; and (5) a prominent position, either unique or shared with other churches, within the religious field of its society.

When a religious system, through a long historical process, comes to be a church, as defined just above, this system tends to perform conservative functions with regard to the internal social structure of the class society in which it functions. This does not mean that it cannot perform "revolutionary" functions in certain circumstances, during certain periods of time, for certain social fractions. No, we are only saying that a church *tends*, the greater part of the time, to perform a conservative function, especially in class societies with a structure of dominance consolidated in a process that has been going on for several generations. This is all the more likely if this church has itself been present as a church during the process of consolidation of that structure of domination.

Why is this so, and how?

One of the sociological characteristics of the type of religious system we have agreed to call "church" is that it can count on a massive, stabilized, and stratified public. To the extent that the force and capacity for social legitimation residing in any religious system—and *a fortiori* in a church—resides precisely in its public, any church will have an interest in preserving that public and in renewing the religious bonds it has with it. But to the extent that this public, being massive and stratified, harbors internal conflicts, at least in latent fashion, to this same extent an ecclesiastical interest in preserving this public will lead to the production of a religious discourse sufficiently ambiguous to satisfy all social fractions, as they make their demands, and to prevent the massive defection of sectors of any social class, dominant or subordinate.

Ambiguous Religious Discourse

Under such conditions, any church will tend to produce a *unitive* and *ambiguous* religious discourse. Almost inevitably, one of its conservative functions will be *symbolically to conceal, displace,* and *transcend* the social conflicts inherent in every class society.

It is sociologically impossible, in conditions of social stability and consolidation of a social structure of dominance, for a church systematically and exclusively to produce a socio-politically side-taking and univocal religious discourse. This is impossible simply because the social fraction against whom such discourse were to be issued could then provoke a religious breach that would materially and symbolically weaken this church. But in producing a socio-politically unitive and ambiguous religious discourse, the church fosters the reproduction of established relationships of domination, and therefore socio-politically favors the dominant classes.

This implicit nexus between ecclesiastical interest in preserving its public and the interest of the dominant classes in preserving the social order will be all the more intimate and efficacious to the extent that it remains unnoticed by religious agents and their public, especially the subordinate fractions of this public. Hence this nexus, this conservative function of the church, tends to remain concealed during periods of consolidation of the hegemony of the dominant classes.

But in moments of hegemonic crisis—when the dominant classes lose the collective consent of society to their dominance, and autonomous social movements develop against them—the conservative function of a church may suddenly become visible, as it lends itself to a side-taking and univocal discourse against the social movements opposing domination. This is what happened in Western Europe during the Napoleonic era, the Revolution of 1848, and at other times. The probability of this occurrence is in direct proportion to the length of time the ecclesiastical hierarchy and the dominant classes have continued in a state of mutual penetration.[128]

Conservative Functionality

This conservative function—implicit in the self-perpetuating strategy of any church—operates on at least two levels. On (1) the level of the maintenance of the symbolic order,[129] any church, to the extent that it has an interest in preserving a dominant position in the religious field of its society, has a tendency, when it cannot assimilate or annihilate other religious systems, to keep them in subjection to its own interests and worldview. It thus supports the socio-political interests of the dominant classes in preventing the rise, or at least the further development, of autonomous religious movements incompatible with the social order.

On (2) the level of the inculcation of a hierarchical logic,[130] to the extent that every church has a hierarchical and centralized organization, and an interest in maintaining this structure, the very presence of a church to its public over a long period of time may result in an unconscious interiorization by the faithful of an attitude of respect towards its hierarchy, authority, and centralized power. The church thereby facilitates the submission of the faithful to other social hierarchies—economic, political, military, and so on. And in general it fosters submission to the social structure of established dominance.

As we have said, a church does not *everywhere and always* perform a conservative function in class societies. Nor is a church the only type of religious system that tends to perform this conservative function. The reason why we have singled out this aspect of the sociological functioning of a church is that, of all religious systems, churches, owing to their character as massive, stratified, and dominant in matters of religion, have the most significant and lasting influence (entirely apart from whether this influence is a conservative one or not) on the mentality and behavior of the social groups that have a religious interest. And also because, in Latin America, the eventual conservative functions of religion are carried out by a particular *church*—the Catholic Church.

Symbolic unification—for instance, in the form of official discourse, with its concealment of social conflict—is the predominant way a church, can exercise conservative functions. But a sect, or a religious movement can also do so by cultivating *division* within subordinate classes—divisions that render difficult or impossible any alliance of the dominated against domination. Thus, just as a *religious unification* of dominant and dominated in a single church generally contributes to the *symbolic transcendence* of socio-political conflicts—and hence converges with the hegemonic strategy of the dominators—so also any internal *religious division* of subordinate classes (especially when a religious unification of dominators and dominated is not feasible) may correspond to the interests of the dominant classes. Thus it may be pursued by these, inasmuch as such division effects a *symbolic displacement* of socio-political conflicts.

Impact of Secularization

As a final theoretical reflection on the potentially conservative functions of religions, let us observe that in highly industrialized capitalistic societies the problem of the social functions of religion is of a far greater complexity than in other societies. Thus in Scandinavia, North America, England, and elsewhere, the religious field tends to pass from a monopolistic structure— and an extremely significant position, socio-politically speaking—to a position that is rather secondary, with a competitive structure similar to that of the contemporary commercial market.[131]

Instead of enjoying a solid internal cohesiveness, the religious field will now be characterized by a certain atomization. Instead of being *the* repository of the power of symbolic production, it will now be just one of several social institutions (and not the most important one) having the function of effecting the symbolic reconstruction of collective experience. This is a function it will share with the schools, the mass media, and so on.

In this secularization process[132]—newly underway in Latin America as well—it becomes more and more questionable to speak, as we have been doing, of the macrosocial functions performed by any particular religion, or even by the religious field as such. The influence of religion in highly industrialized society appears to be reduced and dispersed to the point where it becomes extremely difficult to distinguish and assess the degree and meaning of such influence, where indeed it exists.

Chapter Thirty-Three

RELIGION IN THE STRATEGY OF SUBALTERN CLASSES TOWARD AUTONOMY

Religions do not always perform purely conservative functions with respect to conflictive social relationships of dominance. Religions do not necessarily constitute an obstacle to the autonomy of subordinate classes, or to their alliances against domination.[133]

Many religions, in a great number of historically recorded cases, appear to have played a signal role in the struggle of dominated classes against internal or external domination.[134] It is this potential "revolutionary" function of religion that will concern us throughout the rest of this fourth and last part of this book.

Before we take up this material, let us formulate the theoretical hypothesis that will govern our first lines of approach. Then we shall pass to a more extended development, emphasizing certain aspects and implications of this hypothesis—namely, that under determinate social conditions, and in the presence of a determinate internal situation in the religious field, certain religious practices, teachings, and institutions perform, in class societies, a role that is favorable to the autonomous development of certain subordinate classes, and to the reinforcement of their alliances against domination.

Whether a religion actually performs such a "revolutionary" role depends less upon the consciousness and intentions of religious agents than it does upon the objective microsocial and macrosocial conditions in which such agents are operating.

This hypothesis can be particularly interesting for the analysis of certain socio-religious conflicts in societies (or social groups) whose worldview is preponderantly religious. There are communities and social groups for whom the only form—or at least an important form, and on occasion the principal form—of situating and orientating themselves, and acting, in their socio-natural milieu, for whatever reasons, has its reference to supernatural and metasocial forces. When such groups and communities are in subjection to a relationship of dominance—when they find themselves reduced to a sub-

136

ordinate position—they tend, as does any other social group, to develop a strategy of autonomy with respect to this dominance, and to strike alliances against it. That is, they tend to develop an *autonomic strategy*. The development and unfolding of this strategy, in communities and groups whose worldview is preponderantly a religious one, is determined by the *religious conditions* in which this strategy unfolds and deploys itself.

Here the ability of a subordinate class to transform the conditions of its existence, to place obstacles in the way of the hegemonic strategy of dominators, and to grow in strength in order to set up opposition to a dominating social bloc, depends upon its ability to develop a worldview that will be independent of and different from the worldview of the dominant classes. The transformation of the subordinate classes' worldview into one that is autonomous and distinct from that of the dominant classes is the indispensable condition for creating the objective possibility of transforming the material conditions of their own existence, and thereby of ceasing to be subordinate classes.[135]

Thus, for subordinate social groups with a preponderantly religious worldview, the ability to transform their subordinate social condition depends upon their ability to construct a *religious* worldview independent of, different from, and in opposition to the dominant worldview in their society.

If the religious work of which the subordinate classes are both subject and object in a determinate society produces a (communicable and shared) religious worldview capable of situating and orientating these subordinate classes in their social-natural surroundings in a manner that will be autonomous and different from and opposed to the dominant classes, then religious production will tend to perform a revolutionary function.

The *degree of autonomy* of a subordinate class can be analyzed on three levels, distinct and complementary, which can develop by phases (and which can fail to develop at all, or stagnate, or reverse the direction of their development). These three levels are those of (1) the degree of *class consciousness* of a given subordinate class, (2) its degree of *class organization*, and (3) its degree of *class mobilization*.

The possibility of a religion's favorable influence on the autonomic strategy of a subordinate group is not, in spite of what may appear from what we have said, reducible to the level of a worldview. A religion has potential influence at any one or more of the three levels at which the degree of a subordinate class's autonomy can be analyzed.

1. Class Consciousness

We define class consciousness, in subordinate classes, as a dominated group's perception of itself *as* a dominated group distinct from dominating groups.

When class consciousness awakens at all, it does so in a specific degree of development, as a moment in a collective process. In subordinate classes, the minimal degree of class consciousness is a mere implicit consciousness of their *difference* from the dominant classes, without any sentiment of opposition or of possibility of transcending their subordinate position. "Some are rich, some are poor, and that's the way it is." The maximal degree, by contrast, is an explicit consciousness of collective opposition to dominant classes, of rejection of their domination, and of the desire, the possibility, and the decision collectively to surmount this subordinate position.

A religion, under certain conditions, can function as the active medium in a subordinate class's passage from one degree of class consciousness to a higher degree—hence as a channel of the subordinate classes' development of an autonomous consciousness. This is especially a possibility when the religious system of the subordinate classes renders explicit their relationships of dominance, desacralizing the dominant classes and taking up struggles against dominance as struggles inspired by supernatural and metasocial forces.[136]

2. Class Organization

By class organization we understand, in the case of subordinate classes, the continuous existence and periodically repeated collective utilization of spaces and times exclusively common to those in a dominated social position.

When class organization takes place, it does so in a determinate degree, as a phase of a social process. The minimal degree of subordinate class organization occurs as a simple periodic convening of dominated groups in spaces and times *different* from those in which the dominating classes convene—for popular celebrations, for example. The maximal degree, by contrast, takes the form of collective association explicitly orientated toward struggle against domination.

Under certain conditions a religion may function as a channel of autonomous organization in subordinate classes. This is all the more likely if there is a single religious system common to the subordinate classes and distinct from and opposed to the religious system or systems of the dominant classes.[137]

3. Class Mobilization

By class mobilization we mean, as regards subordinate classes, collective actions of explicit confrontation with the power of dominant classes.

Class mobilization, too, when it takes place, does so at a determinate degree—and as an *expression* (hence, in this case, more than a mere moment)—of a social process. The minimal grade of class mobilization consists in spontaneous and discontinuous actions of protest, merely local actions expressing the demands of isolated groups. The maximal degree consists in systematic and continuous actions of a gradually accelerating offensive against domination. These actions have a political reach, tending to broadening and deepening the transformatory capacity of the subordinate classes—that is, their *power.*

Under certain conditions a religion can also function as a channel of the mobilization of subordinate classes against domination. This is all the more likely if there are declared, overt conflicts between one religious system, common to the subordinate classes, and another that is exclusive to dominant classes.

Chapter Thirty-Four

RELIGIOUS AUTONOMY AND REVOLUTIONARY STRATEGY

In some communities, as in some feudal societies, the religious field constitutes the principal institution for the reproduction of social relationships. In such societies it is practically impossible to undertake a struggle for the transformation of these relationships in the absence of significant antecedent or simultaneous mutations in the religious sphere.

This is all the more true if the groups capable of taking a transformatory initiative have a preponderantly religious worldview. In this case the class consciousness of these groups, their awareness of their difference, subordination, opposition, and conflict vis-à-vis dominators, is necessarily a religious awareness.

In other words, these groups will not be able to develop their class consciousness without religious mediation—that is, without religious changes permitting them to situate and orientate themselves differently from the dominators and in open opposition to their domination (which will in turn open to them the possibility of acting against the domination). Only in the antecedent or concomitant presence of religious transformations can such groups situate and orientate themselves, and act, in opposition to dominant classes.[138]

In other types of societies, such as in capitalism, where the religious field does *not* constitute the principal reproductive institution of social relationships, there nevertheless exist social groups whose worldview is preponderantly religious. In these types of societies, religious changes are not always necessary for social transformations. There can be significant social changes without the production of any innovation or mutation in the religious sphere.

However, in these societies as well, the subordinate classes whose worldview is preponderantly religious will have difficulty taking any initiatives or participating in a process of transformation of society unless its religious worldview undergoes appropriate transformations. Even in these societies, then, the classes in question will be unable to develop their class consciousness without religious mediation.

Innovation and Autonomy

In these two types of situations, certain subordinate classes—the ones with a preponderantly religious worldview—will have an interest in developing a certain *religious autonomy* vis-à-vis the dominating classes, in order to be able to situate and orientate themselves, and to act, against the domination.

By the religious autonomy of certain subordinate classes, we mean the development in these classes of a religious worldview different from and opposed to the hegemonic worldview of the governing classes. But this is not enough. For subordinate classes to manage to gain religious autonomy vis-à-vis dominating classes, their worldview must be one that will enable them to perceive themselves as subordinate classes in opposition to dominant classes, and desirous of, capable of, and driven to surmounting their own subordinate condition by transforming the relationships of domination.

But, as we have already suggested, religious autonomy of these subordinate classes is impossible without religious innovation—without mutations in the religious sphere. Why? Simply because the maintenance of a traditional religious view under the hegemony of a bloc of governing classes can orientate those who share it only toward the preservation of what is traditional—toward the preservation of the established social order.

In order for a subordinate class to be able to place itself in opposition to the domination of a hegemonic bloc of governing classes, it is necessary that it resituate and reorientate itself in its socio-natural surroundings. If this subordinate class has a preponderantly religious worldview, it will be necessary for it to revise its religious worldview. There is no other way for it to resituate and reorientate itself vis-à-vis the governing classes in a novel stance.[139] And this revision of its religion will be the result of the innovation or mutation that we have stated to be indispensable if certain subordinate classes are to become religiously autonomous vis-à-vis the governing classes of their society.

Not every religious innovation, however, constitutes a dynamizing element for the religious autonomy of subordinate classes. On the contrary, many mutations of the religious sphere constitute simple adaptive transformations, or even transformations that intensify the situation of dominance.

Further, certain religious innovations, generated originally within the autonomic strategy of certain subordinate classes, can, as they proceed, give way to a rejective disqualification (a socio-political marginalization) of the subject group. They will, consequently, occasion the fragmentation and debilitation of the subordinate classes. This occurs especially when the religious innovation constitutes a breach with the religious traditions of the subordinate classes (and transgresses the limits of tolerance of the dominant culture), of such a magnitude that the massive reaction of the subordinate classes is necessarily one of incomprehension, rejection, and marginalization of the innovation, instead of collective mobilization in pursuit of it.

In order that a religious innovation actually constitute a dynamizing element for the religious autonomy of a subordinate class, such innovation, in addition to having the antihegemonic traits already alluded to, must also succeed in preserving a certain *continuity* with the traditions of that class—especially with its *religious traditions*. Only such continuity can render possible the communication, diffusion, and acceptance of this religious innovation, and generate a collective mobilization in pursuit of it.

And yet these same antihegemonic traits, indispensable for the purpose of allowing a religious innovation to contribute to the religious autonomy of a subordinate class, imply a certain *breach* with religious tradition—that is, with hegemonic religious traditions. Only such a breach can permit the innovation to become an element of differentiation and opposition on the part of the subordinate classes with respect to the dominant ones. This breach can consist in anything from the birth of a tendency internal to a monopolistic church all the way to the development of an ecclesiastical *schism*.

Autonomy from within Diverse Religious Systems

In societies with a single religious system common to dominators and dominated, the religious autonomy of subordinate classes can develop either out of the constitution of a strong antihegemonic tendency within the existing religious system, or out of a schism capable of separating dominators from dominated in two different and opposing systems as far as religion is concerned.

In societies with a religious system proper to the subordinate classes and distinct from that of the dominant ones, the religious autonomy of the subordinate classes can be consolidated by the development of antihegemonic tendencies already implicit in the mere fact of the existence of a religious system proper to these classes—common to them and exclusive of the dominators, as in the case of French Algeria.

Then there are societies in which the subordinate classes are internally divided by the presence of various religious systems. Their religious autonomy requires, as happened in Vietnam, the development of certain elements common to the subordinate public of each of the religions present—elements permitting the striking of an alliance among these groups (in spite of their religious differences) and their *united* opposition to the dominant classes.

As we can appreciate, however necessary a condition religious autonomy may be for overcoming a situation of subordination, this autonomy is not always possible. And when it is possible, its avenues of realization vary from society to society, class to class, time to time, and religion to religion. In all cases where such autonomy is possible, however, a certain compromise must be struck between *continuity* with tradition, and *breach* with domination, in order to actually contribute to the antihegemonic struggle of the oppressed.

Chapter Thirty-Five

POTENTIAL REVOLUTIONARY FUNCTION OF CHURCH SYSTEMS

Every church—understanding "church" in the sociological sense we defined above (Chapters Twenty-Four and Thirty-Two)—conceals internal conflicts. Under certain circumstances they may develop in such a way as to foster religious processes with nonconservative, even revolutionary, social functions.

The possibility of a church's performing functions favorable to the autonomy of subordinate classes, and hence contrary to certain forms of social dominance, is especially prominent in cases where a society is invaded by foreign groups with religious beliefs different from their own. In such circumstances, if a majority of the invaded belong to a single church, the reaction of this church against the imposition of a foreign culture will contribute to the strengthening of movements of national liberation on the part of the invaded. A case in point would be that of Catholic Poland, several times in recent centuries, and today.

But in cases of social movements against certain forms of internal dominance, as well—in the interior of a society—processes can develop within a church, to which both dominated and dominators belong, that will be favorable to the autonomy of the subordinate classes. When all other socially possible forms of protest against economic, political, cultural, or other forms of domination are blocked by central power, as today in El Salvador, Guatemala, Chile, Argentina, and so on, the likelihood increases that the discontent of the subordinate classes may invade the church, and find religious expression in this church.

This likelihood is enhanced in the case where the church has loosened its ties with central power. In such circumstances, if popular discontent finds an echo in the church, it is probable that the protest will succeed in organizing and developing through that church, to emerge in a collective and prolonged movement of struggle against dominance.

143

Here it is to be observed that in Latin America the Catholic priest has often become a sort of *organic intellectual* for certain of the subordinate classes. That is, he has become a (religious) functionary spontaneously sought out by the masses for the purpose of gathering, systematizing, expressing, and making response to the aspirations and needs of these subordinate classes. Hence the priest can play a key role in these sectors' struggles and alliances.

The potential revolutionary function of certain categories of clergy having ties with subordinate sectors tends to manifest itself, generally as a minority, in social crises. This is all the more likely when the ties of the church in question with the dominant sectors become loosened and the crisis is prolonged, to the accompaniment of the evolution of social movements.

The potential revolutionary function of certain groups of clergy is more likely to be actualized where (1) the subordinate sectors linked to them make religious demands whose content is markedly autonomous and antihegemonic, and (2) where the church itself is the seat of new theological developments favorable to the autonomy of subordinate classes.

Here it is to be noted that theological transformations exercise an impact on the worldview of subordinate sectors especially through liturgy and preaching. That is, such theological impact is exerted through the channels through which religious production is conveyed to the intellectually dominated social fractions of the lay public.

The ever more numerous instances of Catholic priests who, beginning with Father Camilo Torres, have functioned in Latin America as prophets (in the sociological sense, as discussed above, in Chapter Twenty-Five), are abundantly illustrative of this possibility. To my way of thinking, the reasons why these priests have been able to mold and mobilize vast middle and popular sectors, with significant antihegemonic impact, are as follows:

1. These priests have collected, systematized, and expressed a set of new, unsatisfied religious demands on the part of the middle and popular sectors of various regions of our continent.

2. They have functioned in a situation of socio-political crisis and flagrant repression by central power. This situation has blocked other channels of expression of popular discontent and has left religious institutions as its only channel.

3. They have been situated in a church in crisis, which has seen its material power and cultural influence eroding. It has been less and less sought after (and privileged) by the organs of economico-political power. And it has witnessed the progressive diminution of its public and its body of ministers.

4. They have conveyed to the subordinate classes of the continent a series of innovations, produced in the Catholic Church since the pontificate of Pope John XXIII, favoring the development of a Catholic worldview *opposed* to the relationships of dominance that prevail in Latin America, but capable of preserving *continuity* with the religious traditions of Latin American popular classes. Hence these innovations could function as religious

channels for *alliances* among the various social sectors oppressed by their dependency and by capitalist industrialization.

As we can gather from what has been said in this final chapter, the social function of the Catholic Church in particular, and of religion in general, in Latin America is not the same in all circumstances. On the contrary, this function is rather a heterogeneous and variable *set* of multiple and conflictive functions, whose future development is difficult to foresee.

As product, terrain, and active factor with regard to social conflicts on our continent, the religious field—and the Catholic Church in particular—constitutes one of the dimensions in which Latin American society, usually without knowing it, is today deciding, from a point of departure in its past, the possibilities, the limits, and the orientations of its immediate future.

AFTERWORD

It has always been difficult for me to draw up the conclusions of any of my studies—mainly because I feel my work to be intrinsically *unfinished* in a threefold sense.

First of all, I view it as provisional, conjectural, and partial—in both senses of this last term. Thus it is subject to revision and correction, to discussion, and to confrontation with other theories as well as with the reality to which these theories refer.

Secondly, I have the presentiment that I shall have to complement this investigation with another—and that one with still another, and so on until the end of my days.

Thirdly, this work arises out of practical political concerns, which overflow both theory and my own individuality. These are concerns to which my writings seek to contribute the bare beginnings of a theoretical response. But by that very fact they will demand release from the confinement of paper and academic discussion, so that the consistency and applicability of my formulations may be tested against historical practice.

This being the case, I can scarcely undertake to draw conclusions from what I have written in this book.

Thus this Afterword will merely meet the minimum requirement of confessing that, for its author, this work is but another incomplete investigation. I have tried to develop here a radical reformulation of the Marxist theory of religion, with a view to beginning to sketch the outlines of a response to some questions arising out of a malaise of mine.

Since 1965, I have been troubled by the existence of certain Latin American societies in which the majority of human beings are subjected to a harsh regimen organized to fatten the bank accounts of local and foreign minorities. This troubles me to the point of incapacitating me for any understanding or living of my gospel faith except by involvement in the struggle against this social regimen, which I perceive as unjust *and* transformable. And it troubles me to the point where I cannot submissively cross my arms in the face of certain allegedly "Christian" attitudes and traditions that appear to me to be an antievangelical instrumentalization of the church in the service of social injustice.

Such is the malaise that has burdened me for over seventeen years. I have already formulated the questions it gives rise to, at the very beginning of this essay: How and why have Latin American church and society arrived at their present situation? What changes are possible in this situation? How can these changes actually be brought about? And this book has been an attempt at some manner of reponse to these questions. But it has been a purely theoretical attempt, undertaken from a strictly sociological viewpoint, and dealing with only one aspect of the problem.

This is why this investigation is incomplete—because now we must move from theory to empirical research, and to socio-political intervention, in order to verify the reach, the limits, and the validity of my propositions. Then too, this sociological perspective must now be broadened and completed with psychological, theological, and other perspectives, until we have covered some of the other dimensions of the infinitely rich phenomenon of religion. Finally, even in a merely sociological perspective, there are other aspects of the religious phenomenon that could not be included in my analysis.

In a certain sense I could wish for this book to represent the conclusion of my Louvain research in Marxist theory of religion. When I began to write it I imagined that what I would write would include a reformulation of this *theory*, corrected and expanded to respond to three basic concerns of Latin American Catholics: (1) to *know* our church and society, (2) to *understand* how and why they have arrived at the situation facing them today, and (3) to learn what the *possibilities for change* are. That is, to come to see what can be done to bring about, within the range of changes possible, the transformations that seem to be the most desirable. But is this what I have actually managed to do, in the four parts of this book? I am not altogether sure.

At times, in rereading what I have written, I have the impression that it is something too much my own, something in which a Marxist theory of religion is no more than a remote and obscure point of departure, reappearing from time to time in one connection or another. (All the better, perhaps?) Then at other times my manuscript looks like a potpourri of other persons' leftovers, with a cohesiveness more artificial than real, lacking the required historical and bibliographical apparatus, lacking the examples that would have made its reading more vivid and realistic, and lacking a clear applicability to contemporary socio-political reality.

The last time I worked out an outline for my book, I had two more parts in mind, which would have been Parts V and VI: one of the problems of empirical research in Latin American sociology of religions, and the other on the problems of socio-political intervention in the Latin American religious field. Basically what I wanted to do with these two parts was point up certain aspects of the problems of socio-political intervention in Latin America. That is, I wanted to suggest how we might *move from theory to practice*, both in the area of scientific research and in that of socio-political intervention.

Both parts have remained unwritten, and perhaps I shall never write them. When the moment came to bring together some conclusions, I nearly had the courage to move into the area of these final two parts—but not enough. Still, my frustrated intentions—frustrated for the time being, at least—may yet provide a framework for the sense and meaning of my book, and at the same time shape my thoughts for this Afterword (which is "final" only in a rhetorical sense).

Up to a certain point, I have done what I wished to do. I wished to offer a theoretical reconstruction of the genesis, structure, and social functions of the religious field in a society of conflictive relationships among social classes such as that of Latin America. But the point of my efforts of theoretical reconstruction would be in those last two nonexistent parts!

I am very far from being a "pure theorist," in spite of my philosophical background. For me, the sense and value of a theoretical reconstruction are expressed in the concept I referred to at the beginning of this book: to *understand* the reality I speak about. But "to understand is to be able to remake," to become personally capable of taking an effective part in the transformation of the reality that troubles one and, because it troubles one, demands that one come to know it in order to transform it.

Thus, if this book is good for anything, within the framework of my conscious and explicit intentions, it could not very well have conclusions. I doubt very much whether the coherence, originality, and documentary basis of a piece of research really has any purpose other than the satisfaction of the academic demand for these same requirements. Meeting them neither demonstrates nor belies the fertility of the underlying research, or its practical, political usefulness. Consequently, they are the last thing in which I would be interested. If this essay happens to fulfill these academic requirements, so much the better. But I do not really much care. What concerns me is whether my theoretical framework is, or is not, helpful for the orientation of enlightening research into the questions that have motivated it, and useful for guiding concrete activity in such a way as to render it efficacious for the transformation of church and society in Latin America.

This is not something that you can know *a priori*, something to be decided by forcing yourself to write conclusions. No; *probo ambulando*. You prove you can move by moving. The "conclusiveness" of our theoretical framework will therefore be demonstrated only *a posteriori*, outside itself—through "militant research" in the form of struggles for the transformation of church and society in Latin America.

And so this book will have no (theoretical) conclusions. It has only this Afterword, inviting the reader to throw open the doors of research and action and not close them, to extend these reflections and not cut them off, to go beyond paper and theory, beyond Marxism and sociology, all the way to the utopia that inspires both Christianity and Marxism: the building of a community of free and autonomous sisters and brothers in full possession of their personhood.

This book can have only one (practical) conclusion: in light of all we have seen, let us move forward once and for all to deeds, and see whether the utopia that has motivated the construction of our theory can become a reality.

NOTES

1. The reference is to the extraordinary incident of August 1976, in Riobamba, Ecuador, where seventeen bishops and more than twenty priests, from all over Latin America, were taken into custody and interrogated about the "subversive meeting" they were conducting. The meeting, in fact, had consisted only in an exchange of pastoral experiences among a group of clergymen who were in solidarity with the hopes and needs of the oppressed in Latin America.

2. The Second General Assembly of CELAM, held in Medellín in 1968, drew up guidelines for a profound change in the church toward solidarity with the poor and oppressed. This important milestone is here branded as a convention of conspirators.

3. The Catholic Church, with full official approbation, recently published a Latin American edition of the Bible that has enjoyed enthusiastic reception and wide distribution. The photographs in it are powerful expressions of everyday life of the Latin American masses, depicting situations of oppression and struggle.

4. This document, along with the two others that follow, is included in a mimeographed collection, "Crisis capitalista e Iglesia en América Latina," published by the Centro de Estudios Ecuménicos, Mexico City, under the direction of Raúl Vidales.

5. *The Rockefeller Report on the Americas* (Chicago: Quadrangle, 1969), p. 31.

6. "Crisis capitalista e Iglesia en América Latina."

7. See Pierre Bourdieu and Luc Boltanski, "Le fétichisme de la langue," *Actes de la Recherche en Sciences Sociales* (Paris) 4 (1975): 2–32.

8. Surprisingly, there is not a single exhaustive study of the concept of religion as used in the "sociology of religions" today.

9. Indeed, one of the criticisms of my *Marxismo y religión* (Caracas: Monte Avila, 1977) is that it does not contain a definition of religion. See Rafael A. Romero, "Comentarios en torno a la obra, *Marxismo y Religión*," *Huella* (Los Teques) 3 (1977): 33.

10. I have a measure of experience, both personal and professional, in the area of religion. I have been an active member of a large number of Catholic organizations for more than eighteen years, and a member of various associations for the sociology of religion.

11. See Irving Copi, *Introduction to Sociology*, 3rd ed. (New York: Macmillan, 1968), chapter 4.

12. Chronologically anterior and axiologically superior, we might say—as well as ontologically anterior and superior (in some degree "other" than the believers themselves and their natural and social milieu).

13. We shall therefore consider a given social phenomenon (discourse, rite, conflict, and so on) "religious" to the extent, and only to the extent, that it has been produced within a complexus of religious practices and teachings, and that it implicitly or explicitly preserves a discernible affirmative reference to such "supernatural" and "superhuman" forces.

14. For a general introductory view to the panorama of sociology—its history, its problems, and its tasks—I recommend Claude Javeau, *Comprendre la sociologie* (Verviers: Marabout, 1976); Peter L. Berger, *Invitation to Sociology: A Humanistic Perspective* (Harmondsworth: Penguin, 1966); and George Lapassade and René Lourau, *Clefs pour la sociologie* (Paris: Seghers, 1971).

15. See Karel Kosik, *Dialéctica de lo concreto* (Mexico City: Grijalbo, 1967) (trans. of Czech original), pp. 25–37; as well as Pierre Bourdieu, Jean-Claude Chamboredon, and Jean-Claude Passeron, *Le métier de sociologue* (Paris-The Hague: Mouton, 1956), vol. 1.

16. See especially Bourdieu et al., *Métier*, pp. 37–41; and texts of Durkheim, Wittgenstein, Claude Bernard, François Simiand, and Marx, ibid., pp. 159–76. See also Gastón Bachelard, *La*

149

formación del espíritu científico (Mexico City-Madrid-Buenos Aires: Siglo XXI, 1975), 4th ed. (trans. from the French), pp. 7-65.
   17. See Javeau, *Comprendre la sociologie*, p. 14. We are indebted to this same work, pp. 13-19, for much of the present chapter.
   18. Ibid., p. 14.
   19. See Alain Touraine, *Pour la sociologie* (Paris: Seuil, 1974), pp. 56, 60-62; also Javeau, *Comprendre la sociologie*, p. 17.
   20. See Berger, *Invitation to Sociology*, passim.
   21. See Chapter Two, above. See also the Introduction of my doctoral dissertation in philosophy "La cuestión religiosa en el Engels premarxista: Estudio de la génesis de un punto de vista en sociología de las religiones" (Louvain: Institut Supérieur de Philosophie, 1976), esp. pp. 45-62.
   22. See, among others, François Houtart and André Rousseau, *L'Eglise face aux luttes révolutionnaires. 1789—Luttes ouvrières du 19me siècle* (Paris-Brussels: Ed. Ouvrières/Vie Ouvrière, 1972), passim. There is an excellent bibliography on our subject at the end of the book; in Eng. see *The Church and Revolution: From the French Revolution of 1789 to the Paris Riots of 1968*, trans. Violet Nevile (Maryknoll, N.Y.: Orbis, 1971).
   23. See "Sociología de la religión y teología: Estudio bibliográfico" (Madrid: Instituto Fe y Secularidad, 1975), *Cuadernos para el Diálogo*, pp. 18 ff.
   24. For Comte, see Paul Arbousse-Bastide, "Auguste Comte et la sociologie religieuse," *Archives de Sociologie des Religions* (Paris) 22 (1966): 3-58. For Marx, see, among other works, my *Marxismo y religión*. For Engels, see my "Engels premarxista." For Saint-Simon, see Pierre Ansart, *Saint-Simon* (Paris: Ed. Universitaires, 1969). For Proudhon, see Pierre Ansart, "Sociologie proudhonienne de la connaissance religieuse," *Contributions à la Sociologie de la Connaissance* (Paris) 1 (1967): 13-33. For a historical survey of the sociology of religion see Instituto Fe y Secularidad, *Sociología de la Religión*; Betty R. Scharf, *The Sociological Study of Religion* (New York: Hutchinson, 1970), chapter 1, "The Sociological Study of Religion: The Pioneers," pp. 13-43; and Joachim Matthes, *Introducción a la sociología de la religión*, vol. 1, *Religión y Sociedad* (Madrid: Alianza, 1971), pp. 9-96 (trans. from the German).
   25. These authors' basic works were written at the beginning of the twentieth century, but their formation dates mainly from the end of the nineteenth. See Max Weber, *The Protestant Ethic and the Spirit of Capitalism* (New York: Scribner's, 1930); Werner Sombart, *The Jews and Modern Capitalism* (London: Unwin, 1913) (trans. from the German); Emile Durkheim, *Elementary Forms of the Religious Life* (New York: Harcourt, Brace, 1968) (trans. from the French); and Ernst Troeltsch, *The Social Teachings of the Christian Churches*, 2 vols. (New York: Harper, 1960) (trans. from the German).
   26. We pass over the fact, by no means negligible for the "underdevelopment" of this discipline in Latin America, that "sociology of religion" was often understood (and many still understand it) as the study of society from the *ecclesiastical* viewpoint—that is, as synonymous with the "social doctrine of the church." See Francisco López Fernández, "Sociedad, ideología y discurso religioso: Marco teórico para el análisis de los mensajes de grupos cristianos de Chile (1970-1973)," licentiate diss. (Louvain: Institut des Sciences Politiques et Sociales, 1976), p. 12.
   27. For example, a decrease in the number of vocations to the priesthood, an increase in departures from the seminary and the priesthood, a diminution in the number of the faithful (celebrating any sacrament, or assisting at Mass), an increasing number of divorces, an increased rate of lay education (demographically and financially), a decrease in the financial receipts of the church, the development of anticlericalism and religious apathy, etc.
   28. López Fernández, "Sociedad," p. 33. This type of sociology is usually termed "religious sociology"—that is, the study of religion in society by and for a religious institution in view of its own particular immediate interests.
   29. See Raúl Vidales and Tokihiro Kudo, *Práctica religiosa y proyecto histórico: Hipótesis para un estudio de la religiosidad popular en América Latina* (Lima: CEP, 1975), pp. 67 ff.
   30. For more details on the history of the sociology of religions in Latin America see López Fernández, "Sociedad," pp. 8-48, also Vidales and Kudo, *Religiosidad popular*, pp. 63-84. Both works, especially the former, contain very fine bibliographical material.
   31. By "sociography" we mean a mere *description* of society, as distinguished from "sociology" in the strict sense, which implies an *explanation* of the society described.
   32. This option has its theological basis in the theology of liberation. See Gustavo Gutiérrez Merino, *A Theology of Liberation: History, Politics, and Salvation* (Maryknoll: Orbis, 1973), as well as the works of Hugo Assmann, Rubem Alves, Enrique Dussel, Leonardo Boff, and others.

33. See my "Marxist Analysis and Sociology of Religion," in *Religion and Social Change: Acts of the 13th Conference* (Lille: CISR, 1975), pp. 397-401, as well as the commentary by Michel Etienne Legrand, "Réflexions épistémologiques d'un psychologue," *Social Compass* (Louvain) 3-4 (1975): 399.

34. For example, substituting the desired for the real, imposing a prefabricated theoretical model upon reality, manufacturing explanations of facts too hurriedly, brushing facts and explanations aside as irrelevant without examining the data sufficiently, etc.

35. This sociology draws on the most recent Latin American scientific reflection on the problem of dependence. See Fernando H. Cardoso, *Cuestiones de sociología del desarrollo en América Latina* (Santiago de Chile: Ed. Universitaria, 1966); Cardoso and Enzo Faletto, *Dependencia y desarrollo en América Latina*, (Mexico City: Siglo XXI, 1971), 4th ed.; Theotonio dos Santos, *Dependencia económica y cambio revolucionario en América Latina* (Caracas: Enseñanza Viva, 1973); André Gunder Frank, "The Development of Underdevelopment," in *Latin America: Underdevelopment or Revolution?* (New York: Monthly Review, 1969); André Gunder Frank, *Capitalism and Underdevelopment in Latin America*, rev. ed. (New York: Monthly Review, 1969); Celso Furtado, *Subdesarrollo y estancamiento en América Latina* (Buenos Aires: EUDEBA, 1966); Pablo González Casanova, *Sociología de la explotación* (Mexico City: Siglo XXI, 1971); Helio Jaguaribe et al., *La dependencia politico-económica de América Latina* (Mexico City-Madrid-Buenos Aires: Siglo XXI, 1973); Ramón Losada Aldana, *Dialéctica del subdesarrollo* (Mexico City: Grijalbo, 1969); Ruy Mauro Marini, *Sousdéveloppement et révolution en Amérique latine* (Paris: Maspero, 1972); Rodolfo Stavenhagen, *Sept thèses erronées sur l'Amérique latine, ou comment décoloniser les sciences humaines* (Paris: Anthropos, 1973); Osvaldo Sunkel and Pedro Paz, *El subdesarrollo latinoamericano y la teoría del desarrollo* (Madrid: Ed. Universitaria; Mexico City: Siglo XXI, 1973).

36. Vidales and Kudo, *Religiosidad popular*, pp. 87-91.

37. In the sense of the "concrete utopia" of the Neo-Marxist German philosopher Ernst Bloch. See his *On Karl Marx* (New York: Seabury, 1971), pp. 159-73; also Laënnec Hurbon, *Ernst Bloch: Utopie et espérance* (Paris: Cerf, 1974).

38. For a most interesting consideration of one of the paths to this type of socialism see Giulio Girardi, "La fábrica como centro de cultura alternativa," *Cuadernos de Educación* (Caracas) 51 (1978): 1-104.

39. One of the more immediate points of departure of this theoretical framework will be found in the recent works of François Houtart. See his "Religion et champ politique: Cadre théorique pour l'étude des sociétés capitalistes périphériques," *Social Compass* 24 (1977): 265-72.

40. François Houtart defines the "religious field" *(champ religieux)* as "that portion of social space constituted by the complexus of religious institutions and agents in [their] interrelationship" (from his "Sociologie de l'Eglise comme institution," course notes, Louvain, 1973, p. 5).

41. This is what the majority of Marxist theoreticians, especially the Leninists, have done in analyzing religious phenomena. See V. I. Lenin, *Acerca de la religión: Recopilación de artículos* (Moscow: Progreso, 1968).

42. This is the other extreme, characteristic of many theologians. Recently I spoke with an Italian priest and theologian who maintains that what produces the most important social transformations is a changed image of God.

43. See note 49, below.

44. This hypothesis originated in the social theory of Karl Marx and Friedrich Engels, and is well presented by Marta Harnecker, *Los conceptos elementales del materialismo histórico* (Mexico City: Siglo XXI, 1973), pp. 74 ff.

45. This concept, like that of "infrastructure," arose within the Marxist sociological tradition. "Mode of production" has sometimes been used to mean the total structure of a society, hence embracing its economic, juridico-political, and ideologico-cultural aspects; but we shall use it here in the strict sense, to denote a "system of organization of a society, with respect to its material resources, in view of producing goods destined for the satisfaction of the needs of the same population."

46. This triple function of the infrastructure of every society was formulated in presentations made in Brussels (1975) and Lyon (1976) by Maurice Godelier. See my sketch of his theories on religion "New Marxist Approaches to the Relative Autonomy of Religion," *Sociological Analysis* 38 (1977): 360.

47. Rather than overload our text with bibliographical apparatus, I refer the reader to the

bibliography in López Fernández, "Sociedad," as well as my "Marxist Analysis and Sociology of Religions: An Outline of International Bibliography up to 1975," *Social Compass* 22 (1975): 401–79.

48. The concept that the form of production—the form of its organization—depends on the content organizable by production itself, seems to be identical with the traditional Marxist assertion that productive forces determine the relationships of production (see Harnecker, *Materialismo histórico*, pp. 50 ff.). However, in Marxist tradition—and this is one of the points upon which we take a critical distance from that tradition—"productive forces" seem not to include the experience, knowledge, habits, and customs of the population concerned (and at times not even the demographic and geographical conditions in which that population is found).

49. In traditional Marxist theory, this too is unclear. Frequently the impression is given that only a single mode of production is possible in each "stage" of the "development of productive forces," and that this mode of production is the ineluctable consequence of that stage of development of productive forces itself. Here again we take our distance, point by point, from the traditional Marxist view of historical development. Maurice Godelier's Preface in Marx-Engels-Lenin, *Sur les sociétés précapitalistes* (Paris: Ed. Sociales/CERM, 1970), pp. 13–142, is of interest. "Structuralism," beginning with the linguistic studies initiated by Ferdinand de Saussure, has developed the much more fruitful hypothesis that human society is a structured reality, and that, as such, it contains various possibilities (finite in number, however) for transformation. In this regard see Claude Lévi-Strauss, *Structural Anthropology* (New York: Basic Books, 1963).

50. Of course there are many other possible classifications of the modes of production, including some that are extraordinarily fruitful for the comparative sociological study of religions. For example, societies can be divided according to their type of production (agrarian, hunting, foraging, etc.), the size of their population (small, large), etc. We shall see something of this below.

51. Pre-Columbian Latin America had both types of societies. The Guaranís of Paraguay belonged to the first (with a communitarian mode of production), the Incas of Peru to the second (with an asymmetric mode). In Latin America today it is evidently the asymmetric modes that prevail, especially one: the *capitalist*. However, certain indigenous and rural communities survive—minoritarian, scattered, and threatened with extinction—retaining characteristics of a traditional communitarian mode of production.

52. This focus corresponds to our particular sociological "option," which we detailed in Part I.

53. In the case of Latin America, the reason for the current prevalence of an asymmetric organization of production should be sought not so much in the Pre-Columbian productive tradition, but in the colonial *imposition*, first, of that organization in semifeudal form by Spain, Portugal, England, France, and Holland—and then, beginning in the nineteenth century, in the neocolonial *imposition* of the asymmetric mode in semicapitalist form by England and, especially, the United States. That is, it is mainly in its external social relationships (with Western Europe and North America) that our Latin American continent has encountered the organizing forces of an asymmetric mode of production.

54. Only in very exceptional cases (nearly always purely individual)in history has there been a conscious renunciation of acquired economic power. The rule, sociologically speaking, is to the contrary.

55. A procedure that is a favorite with Third World Marxists—a very easy, but not very fruitful one—is precisely to neglect the work of reconstruction of the many Pre-Columbian modes of production, which must begin with an empirical investigation. Generally these modes are all assumed to be reducible to one of the prefeudal European modes of production modeled in classical Marxism: primitive communism and slavery. This work of reconstruction has still not been done. And yet it is perhaps only on the basis of this work that we shall be in a position to work out a well-founded theory of the relationships between the area of religion and the social conflicts of Latin America. For now we shall have to content ourselves with this first approach to the problem, some of whose lacunae and insufficiencies are owing to the absence of this work of reconstruction of the Pre-Columbian modes. I can, however, refer the reader to a series of parallel research projects, exemplary in their genre, carried out on other societies with respect to the tributary mode of production and religion's place in that mode: see *Social Compass* 24 (1977): 157–260.

56. Some have suggested in effect that our spontaneous distinction between "religious" institutions and other kinds of institutions is a sort of projection of our own historico-social conditions of existence, in which activity socially considered religious is performed at places and times, and with a personnel and special traits, that *visibly* differentiate it from economic, politi-

cal, military, scientific, and other activities. See Samir Amin, *Elogio de socialismo* (Barcelona: Anagrama, 1974), pp. 9 ff.; also my "Engels premarxista," pp. 56–64. Notice, by the way, this example of how social conditions influence our perception of religion.

57. For example, in such communities we shall look in vain for distinct religious "disciplines" or practices, complex and diversified liturgy, or complicated theological or moral tractates full of divisions and subdivisions. Sociological attention to this phenomenon began with Max Weber, *Economy and Society: An Outline of Interpretive Sociology* (New York: McGraw-Hill, 1970), pp. 399–634. Later work was done by Pierre Bourdieu, "Genèse et structure du champ religieux," *Revue Française de Sociologie* (Paris) 12 (1971): 301–8.

58. See Bourdieu, "Champ religieux," pp. 301–8.

59. See Emile Durkheim, *Divisions of Labor in Society* (New York: Free Press, 1947).

60. See my "Peasant Religious Symbolism: Its Relative Autonomy," in *Religious-Secular Symbolism and Social Classes: Acts of the 14th Conference* (Lille: CISR, 1977), pp. 352 ff.

61. A monopoly that, however, has never succeeded in becoming total. Just at the moment of the greatest religious monopoly of the Catholic Church, in the sixteenth century, the Protestant Reformation shook Europe, and sabotaged the Catholic unification of that continent. See, among others, Leszek Kolakowski, *Chrétiens sans église: La conscience réligieuse et le lien confessionel au XVIIᵉ siècle* (Paris: Gallimard, 1969).

62. See Maurice Godelier, "Marxisme, anthropologie et religion," in *Epistémologie et marxisme* (Paris: 10/18, 1972), pp. 209–65; Hugues Portelli, *Gramsci y la cuestión religiosa* (Barcelona: Laia, 1977), pp. 58–64; also my "Autonomy of Religion." Below we shall see this same question from another viewpoint, and this will afford us an opportunity to clarify our position on it.

63. See Chapter Two, above.

64. See Pierre-Philippe Rey, *Las alianzas de clases* (Mexico City-Madrid-Buenos Aires: Siglo XXI, 1976), pp. 16 ff.

65. See Chapter Nine, above.

66. This hypothesis, according to which, in a class society, the interpretation of a single religious message varies with the social position of each group receiving the message, is of Marxist origin: see Karl Marx and Friedrich Engels, *On Religion* (New York: Schocken, 1964). We think this hypothesis needs to be critically nuanced, in accordance with observations that we shall develop below and based especially on the reflections of Antonio Gramsci and Pierre Bourdieu. For a most interesting approach, on a more general level, to how class status conditions possibilities, impossibilities, and tendencies in a group or individual presented with a statement of information, see Lucien Goldmann, "Importancia del concepto de conciencia posible para la comunicación," in *El concepto de información en la ciencia contemporánea* (trans. from the French) (Mexico City: Siglo XXI, 1970), pp. 31–54. For a theoretical reflection on the problem on the level of the sociology of religions, see López Fernández, "Sociedad," pp. 152–55.

67. See Alaine Touraine, *Production de la société* (Paris: Seuil, 1973), pp. 145 ff.

68. In principle, the ascent, descent, or stationary condition of the trajectory of an individual or fraction of society is measurable by comparison with the preceding generation (of the individual's family or the fraction's group of families), using, among other criteria, the economico-political dimensions delineated in Chapter Eight and note 46, above.

69. See Pierre Bourdieu, "Avenir de classe et causalité du probable," *Revue Française de Sociologie* 15 (1974): 3–42.

70. Let us take an example. There would not be the same religious necessities in a working-class neighborhood of peasant origin, with a descending trajectory (marginalization), an unfavorable relative conjuncture, and a transactional submission strategy, as in a working-class neighborhood originating in the working class itself, with an ascending trajectory (modernization), a favorable conjuncture, and a strategy of demand for reform. Very probably, for instance (in just one aspect of the question), the former would be fairly receptive to an approach by religious sects such as the Jehovah Witnesses, whereas the latter would be extremely resistant to any religious system of an apocalyptic type. See, among many others, Vittorio Lanternari, *Les mouvements religieux des peuples opprimés* (Paris: Maspero, 1962).

71. See esp. Nicos Poulantzas, *Political Power and Social Classes* (New York: Humanities, 1975); Georges Gurvitch, *El concepto de clases sociales de Marx a nuestros días* (Buenos Aires: Nueva Visión, 1967); Stanislas Ossowski, *Class Structure in the Social Consciousness* (New York: Free Press, 1963); Theotonio dos Santos, *El concepto de clases sociales* (Bogotá: Universidad Nacional, 1970).

72. See Hugues Portelli, *Gramsci e il blocco storico* (Bari: Laterza, 1973), pp. 67–100.

73. See Touraine, *Production*, pp. 145 ff.

74. For an interesting analysis of how Catholicism underwent important modifications first under feudalism and then under capitalism, see Portelli, *Gramsci y la cuestión religiosa*, and our review of the same in "New Marxist Approaches."

75. This seems to us to be the most fertile contribution of Marxist criticism to the sociology of religions, and we have attempted to systematize it as such in our *Marxismo y religión*.

76. See my "Introduction," *Social Compass* 22 (1975): 313 ff.

77. See Portelli, *Gramsci y la cuestión religiosa*; Lanternari, *Mouvements*.

78. See the interesting work of François Houtart, *Religion and Ideology in Sri Lanka* (Bangalore: TPI, 1974).

79. We are largely dependent in Part III on the extraordinary article of Pierre Bourdieu already cited, "Gènese et structure du champ religieux." Hence we shall but rarely make explicit reference to it. We shall, however, generally cite Bourdieu's other articles.

80. See Jean Piaget, *Biology and Knowledge: An Essay on the Relations between Organic Regulations and Cognitive Processes* (Chicago: Univ. of Chicago, 1971), especially pp. 333–45.

81. See Leszek Kolakowski et al., *Le besoin religieux* (texts of addresses and meetings organized by Rencontres Internationales de Genève, 1973) (Boudry-Neuchâtel: Baconnière, 1974).

82. The explanation offered by a static theology—the "religious necessity" supposedly inherent in every human being—like the atheistic-evolutionary one of an "inferior degree of development" of certain societies or social groups (the latter being the one shared by the majority of Marxists) are each as undemonstrable as they are irrefutable. Worse, they explain nothing. That is, they "explain" everything *a priori*, hence are perfectly useless as hypotheses for explaining the differences and transformations of religion in comparison with differences and changes of the macro- and microsocial contexts under consideration.

83. See López Fernández, "Sociedad," p. 141; also Douglas F. Barnes, "Charisma and Religious Leadership: An Historical Analysis," *Journal for the Scientific Study of Religion* (New York) 17 (1978): 1–18.

84. See Louis Althusser, *Positions (1964–1975)* (Paris: Ed. Sociales, 1976), pp. 105–9 ("Idéologie et appareils idéologiques d'état: Notes pour une recherche").

85. See Jean Remy, Jean-Pierre Hiernaux, and Emile Servais, "Formes religieuses en transformation: Rapport à l'ordre social et aux structures symboliques," *Conférence Internationale de Sociologie Religieuse: Changement social et religion: Actes de la 13e Conférence* (Lille: CISR, 1975), pp. 87–110.

86. See Bourdieu, "Champ religieux," p. 305.

87. Of course in some Pre-Columbian cultures there was a certain specialization of religious work, with functionaries specifically charged with duties such as offering sacrifices. In these cases what Luso-Hispanic colonialism strove for was the conversion or replacement of these functionaries—intensifying the existing division of labor—and the imposition of Catholicism as the new religion of these cultures.

88. Unlike what Marxist theory of religion had traditionally held.

89. See López Fernández, "Sociedad," p. 141.

90. Bourdieu, in his "Champ religieux," seems to reduce the basis of the (relative) autonomy of religion to this last dimension, not only forgetting that this institutional trait, unlike the other two, is not present in all religions, but also neglecting the fact that the last trait seems possible only given the other two.

91. Obviously the number of members and the diversity of the social fractions covered by a specialized body of religious functionaries can complicate this structure of domination, to the degree that obtains in the Catholic Church today.

92. See Weber, *Economy and Society,* pp. 399–634; Bourdieu, "Champ religieux," p. 305.

93. For example, in predominantly Catholic countries the demands of industrial youth will be transmitted to the religious area via religious institutions like the JOC (*Juventud Obrera Católica*, Young Catholic Workers).

94. Besides, prolonged *contact* between a category of clergy and a particular social fraction (independently of any structural homology of social position, or common social origin, between the two groups—in fact, even in spite of their mutual disparity in these respects) can act as a mechanism of development of a certain *openness* in this category of clergy to the religious demands of this particular social fraction, as well as a resistance to the religious demands of social fractions in conflict with it. Of course there are myriads of other factors as well (family, psychological, intellectual, etc.) that can occasion the development of such openness and reticence, even in the face of factors that can seem more relevant sociologically. Nevertheless, the *dominant*

tendency seems to us to be the one we have described in the text, especially in the long term and across the total social scale.

95. See François Houtart, "Champ religieux et champ politique dans la société singhalaise," *Social Compass* 20 (1973): 105–38.

96. See Leon Festinger et al., *When Prophecy Fails: A Social and Psychological Study of a Modern Group that Predicted the Destruction of the World* (New York: Harper & Row, 1956).

97. See Portelli, *Gramsci y la cuestión religiosa*, pp. 141–48. The complexity of the position and structure of a church leads it—strategically—to produce three types of theoretical elaboration, according to Gramsci: *organic* (corresponding to the asymmetric religious demand of the laity in a specific social structure), *organizational* (corresponding to the internal needs of religious institutions as such), and *conjunctural* (corresponding to provisional exigencies arising from unforeseen social situations that threaten the stability of ecclesiastical institutions). See also pp. 163–67.

98. Or, to put it in the terminology of linguistics, the prophet is that person (or group) who is capable of joining an already existing *signifier* to a *significate* that lacks a signifier (the unsatisfied demand), thus constructing a new *sign*, which—unlike a *mere* sign—is also the mobilizing *symbol* of the individual and collective energies of the bearers of the significate.

99. See Jean Remy, "Innovations et développement des structures: Les problèmes que pose l'institutionalisation," *Lumen Vitae* (Brussels) 2 (1969): 201–28; Juan Estruch, *La innovación religiosa: Ensayo teórico de sociología de la religión* (Barcelona: Ariel, 1972).

100. In this connection see the treatment of the theology of liberation by Gustavo Gutiérrez, *A Theology of Liberation: History, Politics, and Salvation* (Maryknoll: Orbis, 1973); Hugo Assmann, *Theology for a Nomad Church* (Maryknoll: Orbis, 1976); and Rubem A. Alves, *A Theology of Human Hope* (Washington, D.C.: Corpus, 1969). On Christians for Socialism see Alfredo Fierro and Reyes Mate, *Cristianos por el Socialismo: Documentación* (Estella [Navarra]: Verbo Divino, 1975); Pablo Richard, *Cristianos por el socialismo: Historia y documentación* (Salamanca: Sígueme, 1976); and Giulio Girardi, *Cristianos por el socialismo* (Barcelona: Laia, 1977). The theology of liberation and Christians for Socialism are the most recent and most significant of the prophetic movements that have arisen in the area of Latin American religion.

101. For instance, suspension *a divinis* (prohibition from celebrating Mass or sacraments), and explusion from the Salesians, were among the penalties imposed on the Italian priest Giulio Girardi, who represented the Christians for Socialism movement in western Europe.

102. See Alain Touraine, *La conscience ouvrière* (Paris: Seuil, 1966), pp. 311 ff., cited and commented upon in Imelda Vega-Centeno Bocangel, "Campo político—campo religioso—luchas populares y coyuntura en el Peru—Estudio de un conflicto laboral en al año 1971," licentiate diss. (Louvain: Institut des Sciences Politiques et Sociales, UCL, 1976), pp. 56 ff. See also Karl Marx, "El Dieciocho Brumario de Luis Bonaparte," in Marx and Friedrich Engels, *Obras escogidas en dos tomos* (Moscow: Progreso, 1966), vol. 1, p. 233; Eng.: *Eighteenth Brumaire of Louis Bonaparte* (New York: International Pubs. Co., 1963).

103. It is by no means an easy matter to render a sociological judgment on the *success* or *failure* of a prophetic movement. In the first place, the right nuance will have to be found between the two extremes of *relative success* and *total failure*. If we define the "total failure" of a prophetic movement sociologically as its objective and subjective disappearance without having achieved any important transformation of the religious field, then, *e contrario*, we could define its "relative success" as its partial attainment of significant changes in the religious field. But such significant transformations or changes in the religious field would have to be changes in accordance with the interests and expectations of the agents of the prophetic movement (changes that can consist in the diffusion of the innovation, the increase of membership in the movement, influence on religious organizations and their position-takings, a lasting modification of the conduct of a significant sector of the ecclesiastical public, or the transformation of the correlation of dominant/dominated forces in the religious field in favor of the dominated). These changes can extend all the way from a partial modification of the church through replacement of part of its dominant hierarchy, to an across-the-board ecclesiastical schism, as in the paradigmatic case of the Protestant Reformation.

104. See Vega-Centeno, "Luchas populares y conyuntura," p. 27.

105. Perhaps this is one reason, among others, why the sanctions imposed on Archbishop Lefebvre have been less severe than those imposed on Father Girardi—precisely because Archbishop Lefebvre's movement, unlike Father Girardi's, is situationed in the broader, deeper, and older socio-historical trajectory of the Catholic Church—the same trajectory it held in feudal-

ism, side by side with the nobility. Many church analysts forget the importance of *time* in the formation of the structural limits of tolerance to innovation in ecclesiastical institutions. They neglect the fact that transformations are much more easily effected in institutions of recent formation than in institutions that have existed for several centuries.

106. See Bernard Poisson, "Schéma d'analyse de l'organisation religieuse," *Sociologie et sociétés* (Montreal), vol. 1, no. 2 (1969), pp. 147-69.

107. Part IV will lack the depth of documentation shown in the earlier parts of this book. Less work has been done on this aspect of the relationships between the religious field and social conflicts. Here, classic sociology of religions has held fast in a rather unilateral position, seeing religion—at most—as a stabilizing factor in the social structure, from pragmatist William James (*Varieties of Religious Experience* [New York: Macmillan, 1961]) to Marxist V. I. Lenin (*Acerca de la religión*). The only radical difference between Marxism and the other sociological theories of religion in this respect is that Marx and Lenin consider the conservative character of religion as an obstacle that can be overcome, whereas the other classical sociologists consider it as positive and insuperable. But as Robert K. Merton has pointed out (*Social Theory and Social Structure* [New York: Free Press, 1968], pp. 38-46), all agree in perceiving religion as a factor of social stabilization. Rarely do they go along with Antonio Gramsci (see Portelli, both works on Gramsci) beyond this perspective. For our own part we shall seek to go beyond this focus—without, however, denying its contributions. In this task it seems to me important to continue the work begun by Gramsci and Bourdieu, as I have suggested in my "New Marxist Approaches."

108. See Touraine, *Production de la société,* passim.

109. But in their own turn, the social relationships established among human beings limit and orientate the worldview that these human beings can develop, as the sociology of knowledge of Karl Mannheim has demonstrated (*Ideology and Utopia: An Introduction to the Sociology of Knowledge* [New York: Harcourt, Brace, Jovanovich, 1955]). See Kurt Lenk, ed., *Ideologie: Ideologiekritik und Wissenssoziologie* (Neuwied-Berlin: Luchterhand, 1971); Alberto Izzo, ed., *Il condizionamento sociale del pensiero* (Turin: Loescher, 1970); and Irving Louis Horowitz, ed., *Historia y elementos de la sociología del conocimiento,* 2 vols. (Buenos Aires: EUDEBA, 1964): three magnificent anthologies on the sociology of knowledge. We might say that what happens is that there is a constant interaction between any collectivity's worldview and its social relationships—a kind of reciprocal conditioning, in which neither the worldview nor the relationships are static, or even passive or inert.

110. See López Fernandez, "Sociedad," p. 50.

111. See Mircea Eliade, *The Sacred and the Profane: The Nature of Religion* (New York: Harcourt, Brace, 1968).

112. See Peter L. Berger and Thomas Luckmann, *The Social Construction of Reality: A Treatise in the Sociology of Knowledge* (Garden City, N.Y.: Doubleday, 1967); likewise Peter Berger, *The Sacred Canopy: Elements of a Sociological Theory of Religion* (Garden City, N.Y.: Doubleday, 1969).

113. See Talcott Parsons, *The Social System* (Toronto: Collier-Macmillan, 1964); Merton, *Social Theory*; Bronislaw Malinowski, *Magic, Science and Religion and Other Essays* (New York: Doubleday, 1954).

114. Let us note in passing, with Merton *(Social Theory)*, that, basically, classic Marxist theory coincides with functionalism in defining religion as a social institution tending always to fulfill the same equilibrating function in society ("opium of the people")—playing a destabilizing, revolutionary role only by way of exception.

115. This is a viewpoint maintained in the works we have cited by Godelier, Houtart, and Portelli.

116. See Weber, *Protestant Ethic*; and Anthony Blasi et al., *Toward an Interpretive Sociology* (Washington, D.C.: University Press of America, 1978), Chapter Nine, "Toward Reconstructing a Sociology of Religion," pp. 263-86.

117. Once more, see above, Chapter Sixteen, where we began to develop this first aspect.

118. By "strategy of extended self-perpetuation" we mean the tendency of this type of class to *maintain* itself as dominant, and simultaneously to *extend* its power, its influence, its domination.

119. See Pierre Bourdieu, "Les stratègies matrimoniales dans le système de réproduction," *Annales* (Paris), nos. 4-5 (1972), pp. 1105-27.

120. See Pierre Bourdieu and Jean-Claude Passeron, *La réproduction: Eléments pour une théorie du systèm d'enseignement* (Paris: Minuit, 1970); Charles Suaud, "L'Ecole de la vocation," diss., 2 vols. (Paris: Hautes Etudes, 1975).

121. The situations listed here will, it seems to me, be useful as *suggestions* (and nothing more)

for sociological theory and research on the conservative role of religion in a class society. It would be necessary to determine in each concrete case whether and to what degree discourses and praxis like these indeed perform such a conservative function. For my part I should perhaps make it clear that I think that such praxis and discourses are never necessarily, *in se*, conservative. But they can *function* as conservative—in the case (and only in the case) where they (1) have a systematically reiterated and massively propagated official character, (2) encounter within the same religious system no official production simultaneously counterpoised to them and enjoying the same systematic and massive character, and (3) are efficaciously and positively linked to a hegemonic strategy of the dominant classes within their own context of systematic and massive official propagation.

122. See my "Extracción de plusvalía, represión de la sexualidad y catolicismo en Latinoamérica," *Expresamente* (Caracas) 4 (1978): 33-39.

123. So termed in Blasi et al., *Interpretive Sociology*, p. 266.

124. This second case seems, in part, to be that of the relationships between the bourgeoisie of northern Europe and the Protestant Reformation, beginning in the sixteenth century, when both came into confrontation with then dominant Catholicism. See Weber, *Protestant Ethic*, passim; Portelli, *Gramsci y la cuestión religiosa*, pp. 75 ff.

125. Consider the case of John Hus in Bohemia in the fifteenth century, or that of Thomas Münzer in Germany in the sixteenth. See Josef Macek, ¿*Herejía o revolución? El movimiento husita* (Madrid: Ciencia Nueva, 1967); Ernst Bloch, *Thomas Münzer als Theologe der Revolution* (Frankfurt: Suhrkamp, 1960).

126. Sociology owes its distinction between a church and a sect to Ernst Troeltsch; see Bryan Wilson, *Religious Sects: A Sociological Study* (New York: McGraw-Hill, 1970).

127. See Lanternari, *Mouvements religieux*.

128. In eighteenth-century France nearly 100 percent of Catholic bishops were landowning members of the feudal nobility; see Houtart, Rousseau, *Church and Revolution*, p. 29.

129. See Bourdieu, "Champ religieux," pp. 328 ff.

130. Ibid., pp. 329 ff.

131. Bourdieu, "Champ religieux," had a predecessor in this concept in the interesting article of Peter L. Berger and Thomas Luckmann, "Secularization and Pluralism," *Internationales Jahrbuch für Religionssoziologie* (Cologne-Opladen) 2 (1966): 73-86.

132. See the exhaustive bibliography on this theme in Instituto Fe y Secularidad, *Sociología y teología*, pp. 302-9 ("Sociología de la secularización") and pp. 395 ff. ("Teología de la secularización").

133. A position with regard to which once again I sharply separate myself from the Marxist tradition.

134. See, again, Lanternari, "Mouvements religieux," passim.

135. And vice versa. The possibility of the subordinate classes' transforming their worldview depends on their objective capability of transforming the material conditions of their existence (and on these material conditions of existence themselves). A dialectic of interaction is at work here between these two variables, the "subjective" and the "objective." This is where, I think, the Marxist conception of the unity of theory and practice (see Jürgen Habermas, *Theory and Practice* [London: Heinemann, 1974]) will be useful. Likewise, it is this connection that the Marxist hypothesis seems valid to us—namely, that in capitalism the social class with the greatest objective potential for setting in motion a social revolution is the urban-industrial working class—thanks to the material conditions of its existence. They not only place it in objectively radical opposition to the dominant classes, but at the same time make it possible for this opposition to become a continuous social movement, organized, disciplined, and conscious. The rural and urban petty bourgeoisie, the peasantry, and even the "marginalized" of city and countryside, are not in these enabling material conditions. See Goldmann, "Conciencia posible."

136. See Carlo Prandi, *Religione e classi subalterne* (Rome: Coines, 1977).

137. These can be "religious systems" in a broad sense, as institutionally differentiated organizations, proper to the subordinate classes, within the church—for instance, the JOC (*Juventud Obrera Católica*, Young Catholic Workers). Or they can be religious systems in the strict sense: religions that are exclusively those of the dominated—for instance, in a sense, the Catholic Church in Northern Ireland today.

138. This seems to me the deeper sense of Max Weber's analysis in *Protestant Ethic*.

139. "Orthodox" Marxism will disagree with us here and hold it necessary for this subordinate class to *abandon* its religious worldview, at least in a capitalist society. See Karl Marx and Friedrich Engels, "Critical Assessment of the Work of Cr. F. Daumer, 'Religion of the New Age,' " in *On Religion* (New York: Schocken, 1964), pp. 90-96.

BIBLIOGRAPHY

Althusser, Louis, "Idéologie et appareils idéologiques d'Etat: Notes pour une recherche," in *Positions (1964-1975)* (Paris: Ed. Sociales, 1976).

Alves, Rubem A., *A Theology of Human Hope* (Washington, D.C.: Corpus, 1969).

Amin, Samir, *Elogio del socialismo* (Barcelona: Anagrama, 1974).

Ansart, Pierre, "Sociologie proudhonienne de la connaissance religieuse," *Contributions à la sociologie de la connaissance* (Paris) 1 (1967): 13-33.

———, *Sociología de Saint-Simon* (Barcelona: Península, 1972).

Arbousse-Bastide, Paul, "Auguste Comte et la sociologie religieuse," *Archives de Sociologie des Religions* (Paris) 22 (1966): 3-58.

Assmann, Hugo, *Teología desde la praxis de la liberación: Ensayo teológico desde la América dependiente* (Salamanca: Sígueme, 1973); in Eng. see *Theology for a Nomad Church*, trans. by Paul Burns, (Maryknoll, N.Y.: Orbis, 1976).

Bachelard, Gaston, *La formación del espíritu científico* (Mexico City-Madrid-Buenos Aires: Siglo XXI, 1975).

Barnes, Douglas F., "Charisma and Religious Leadership: An Historical Analysis," *Journal for the Scientific Study of Religion* (New York) 17 (1978): 1-18.

Berger, Peter L., *Invitation to Sociology: A Humanistic Perspective* (Harmondsworth: Penguin, 1966).

———, *The Sacred Canopy: Elements of a Sociological Theory of Religion* (Garden City, N.Y.: Doubleday, 1969).

———, and Luckmann, Thomas, "Secularization and Pluralism," *Internationales Jahrbuch für Religionssoziologie* (Cologne-Opladen) 2 (1966): 73-86.

———, and Luckmann, Thomas, *The Social Construction of Reality: A Treatise in the Sociology of Knowledge* (Garden City, N.Y.: Doubleday, 1967).

Blasi, Anthony, et al., *Toward an Interpretive Sociology* (Washington, D.C.: University Press of America, 1978), pp. 263-86 (chapter 9: "Toward Reconstructing a Sociology of Religion").

Bloch, Ernst, *Thomas Münzer als Theologe der Revolution* (Frankfurt: Suhrkamp, 1960).

———, *Pour Marx* (Paris: Maspero, 1965); English trans., *On Karl Marx* (New York: Seabury, 1971).

Bourdieu, Pierre, "Genèse et structure du champ religieux," *Revue Française de Sociologie* (Paris) 12 (1971): 295-334.

———, "Les stratégies matrimoniales dans le système de reproduction," *Annales* (Paris) 4-5 (1972): 1105-27.

———, "Avenir de classe et causalité du probable," *Revue Française de Sociologie* 15 (1974).

———, and Boltanski, Luc, "Le fétichisme de la langue," *Actes de la Recherche en Sciences Sociales* (Paris) 4 (1975): 2-32.

———, Chamboredon, Jean-Claude, and Passeron, Jean-Claude, *Le métier de sociologie,* vol. 1 (Paris-The Hague: Mouton, 1965).

———, and Passeron, Jean-Claude, *La reproduction: Eléments pour une théorie de système d'enseignement* (Paris: Ed. de Minuit, 1970).

Cardoso, Fernando H., *Cuestiones de sociología del desarrollo en América Latina* (Santiago de Chile: Ed. Universitaria, 1966).

———, and Faletto, Enzo, *Dependencia y desarrollo en América Latina* (Mexico City: Siglo XXI, 1971).

Copi, Irving M., *Introduction to Logic*, 3rd ed. (New York: Macmillan, 1968).

Dos Santos, Theotonio, *El concepto de clases sociales* (Bogotá: Universidad Nacional de Colombia, Departamento de Historia, 1970).

158

————, *Dependencia económica y cambio revolucionario en América Latina* (Caracas: Enseñanza Viva, 1973).

Durkheim, Emile, *Divisions of Labor in Society* (New York: Free Press, 1947).

————, *Elementary Forms of the Religious Life,* trans. by Joseph W. Sevain (New York: Free Press, 1954).

Eliade, Mircea, *The Sacred and the Profane: The Nature of Religion,* trans. by William Trask (New York: Harcourt, Brace, 1968).

Estruch, Juan, *La innovación religiosa: Ensayo teórico de sociología de la religión* (Barcelona: Ariel, 1972).

Festinger, Leon, et al., *When Prophecy Fails: A Social and Psychological Study of a Modern Group that Predicted the Destruction of the World* (New York: Harper & Row, 1956).

Fierro, Alfredo, and Mate, Reyes, *Cristianos por el socialismo: Documentación* (Estella [Navarra]: Ed. Verbo Divino, 1975).

Furtado, Celso, *Subdesarrollo y estancamiento en América Latina* (Buenos Aires: EUDEBA, 1966).

Girardi, Giulio, *Cristianos por el socialismo:* Barcelona: Laia, 1977).

————, "La fábrica como centro de cultura alternativa," *Cuadernos de Educación* (Caracas) 51 (1978): 1–104.

Godelier, Maurice, Preface, in Marx-Engels-Lenin, *Sur les sociétés précapitalistes* (Paris: Ed. Sociales/CERM, 1970), pp. 13–142.

————, "Marxisme, anthropologie et religion," in *Epistémologie et marxisme* (Paris: 10/18, 1972), pp. 209–65.

Goldmann, Lucien, "Importancia del concepto de consciencia posible para la comunicación," in *El concepto de información en la ciencia contemporánea* (Mexico City: Siglo XXI, 1970), pp. 31–54.

González Casanova, Pablo, *Sociología de la explotación* (Mexico City: Siglo XXI, 1971).

Gunder Frank, André, *Capitalism and Underdevelopment in Latin America,* rev. ed. (New York: Monthly Review Press, 1969).

————, *Underdevelopment or Revolution* (New York: Monthly Review Press, 1969).

Gurvitch, Georges, *El concepto de clases sociales de Marx a nuestros días* (Buenos Aires: Nueva Visión, 1967).

Gutiérrez Merino, Gustavo, *A Theology of Liberation: History, Politics and Salvation,* trans. by Sister Caridad Inda and John Eagleson (Maryknoll, N.Y.: Orbis, 1973).

Habermas, Jürgen, *Theory and Practice* (London: Heinemann, 1974); abridged ed., trans. John Viertal (Boston: Beacon, 1973).

Harnecker, Marta, *Los conceptos elementales del materialismo histórico* (Mexico City: Siglo XXI, 1973).

Horowitz, Irving L., ed., *Historia y elementos de la sociología del conocimiento,* 2 vols. (Buenos Aires: EUDEBA, 1964).

Houtart, François, "Sociologie de l'Eglise comme institution," lecture notes (Louvain: UCL, 1973).

————, "Champ religieux et champ politique dans la société singhalaise," *Social Compass* (Louvain) 20 (1973): 105–38.

————, *Religion and Ideology in Sri Lanka* (Bangalore: TPI, 1974).

————, "Religion et champ politique: Cadre théorique pour l'étude des sociétés capitalistes périphériques," *Social Compass* 24 (1977): 265–72.

————, and Rousseau, André, *The Church and Revolution: From the French Revolution of 1789 to the Paris Riots of 1968,* trans. Violet Nevile (Maryknoll, N.Y.: Orbis, 1971).

Hurbon, Laënnec, *Ernst Bloch: Utopie et espérance* (Paris: Cerf, 1974).

Instituto Fe y Secularidad, *Sociología de la religión y teología* (Madrid: Cuadernos para el Diálogo, 1975).

Izzo, Alberto, ed., *Il condizionamento sociale del pensiero* (Turin: Loescher, 1970).

Jaguaribe, Helio, et al., *La dependencia político-económica de América Latina* (Mexico City-Madrid-Buenos Aires: Siglo XXI, 1973).

James, William, *Varieties of Religious Experience* (New York: Macmillan, 1961).

Javeau, Claude, *Comprendre la sociologie* (Verviers: Marabout, 1976).

Kolakowski, Leszek, *Chrétiens sans église: La conscience religieuse et le lien confessionnel au XVIIᵉ siècle* (Paris: Gallimard, 1969).

————, et al., *Le besoin religieux,* texts of conferences organized by the Rencontres Internationales de Genève, 1973 (Boudry-Neuchâtel: Ed. de la Baconnière, 1974).

Kosik, Karel, *Dialéctica de lo concreto,* trans. from the Czech (Mexico City: Grijalbo, 1967).

Lanternari, Vittorio, *Les mouvements religieux des peuples opprimés* (Paris: Maspero, 1962).
Lapassade, Georges, and Lourau, René, *Clefs pour la sociologie* (Paris: Seghers, 1971).
Legrand, Michel, "Réflexions epistémologiques d'un psychologue," *Social Compass* 22 (1975): 397–400.
Lenin, V.I., *Acerca de la religión* (Moscow: Progreso, 1968).
Lenk, Kurt, ed., *Ideologie: Ideologiekritik und Wissenssozologie,* 5th ed. (Neuwied-Berlin: Lunchterhand, 1971).
López Fernández, Francisco, "Sociedad, ideología y discurso religioso: Marco teórico para el análisis de los mensajes de grupos cristianos de Chile (1970–1973)," licentiate diss. (Louvain: Institut des Sciences Politiques et Sociales/UCL, 1976).
Losada Aldana, Ramón, *Dialéctica del subdesarrollo* (Mexico City: Grijalbo, 1969).
Macek, Josef, *¿Herejía o revolución?: El movimiento husita* (Madrid: Ciencia Nueva, 1967).
Maduro, Otto, Introduction to *Social Compass* 22 (1975): 305–22.
——, "Marxist Analysis and Sociology of Religions: An Outline of International Bibliography up to 1975," *Social Compass* 22 (1975): 401–79.
——, "Marxist Analysis and Sociology of Religion," in *Religion and Social Change,* Acts of the 13th Conference, Lloret de Mar (Lille: Secrétariat CISR, 1975), pp. 395–401.
——, "La cuestión religiosa en el Engels premarxista: Estudio de la génesis de un punto de vista en sociología de las religiones," doctoral diss. (Louvain: Bibliothèque de l'Institut Supérieur de Philosophie/UCL, 1976); also published by Monte Avila Editores, Caracas, Venezuela.
——, *Marxismo y religión* (Caracas: Monte Avila, 1977).
——, "Peasant Religious Symbolism: Its Relative Autonomy," in *Religious-Secular Symbolism and Social Classes,* Acts of the 14th Conference, Strasbourg (Lille: Secrétariat CISR, 1977), pp. 349–55.
——, "New Marxist Approaches to the Relative Autonomy of Religion," *Sociological Analysis* (Chicago) 38 (1977): 359–67.
——, "Extracción de plusvalía, represión de la sexualidad y catolicismo en Latinoamérica," *Expresamente* (Caracas) 4 (1978): 33–39.
Malinowski, Bronislaw, *Magic, Science and Religion and Other Essays* (New York: Doubleday, 1954).
Mannheim, Karl, *Ideology and Utopia: An Introduction to the Science of Knowledge* (New York: Harcourt, Brace, Jovanovich, 1955).
Marini, Ruy Mauro, *Sous-développement et révolution en Amérique latine* (Paris: Maspero, 1972).
Marx, Karl, and Engels, Friedrich, *On Religion* (New York: Schocken, 1964).
——, *Obras escogidas en dos tomos* (Moscow: Progreso, 1966).
Matthes, Joachim, *Introducción a la sociología de la religión,* vol. 1 (Madrid: Alianza, 1971).
Merton, Robert K., *Social Theory and Social Structure* (New York: Free Press, 1968).
Ossowski, Stanislas, *Class Structure in the Social Consciousness* (New York: Free Press, 1963).
Parsons, Talcott, *The Social System* (New York: Free Press, 1951).
Piaget, Jean, *Biology and Knowledge: An Essay on the Relations between Organic Regulations and Cognitive Processes* (Chicago: University of Chicago Press, 1971).
Poisson, Bernard, "Schéma d'analyse de l'organisation religieuse," *Sociologie et sociétés* (Montreal) 1 (1969).
Portelli, Hugues, *Gramsci e il blocco storico* (Bari: Laterza, 1973).
——, *Gramsci y la cuestión religiosa* (Barcelona: Laia, 1977).
Poulantzas, Nicos, *Pouvoir politique et classes sociales* (Paris: Maspero, 1970); trans. Timothy O'Hagan, *Political Power and Social Classes* (New York: Humanities Press, 1975).
Prandi, Carlo, *Religione e classi subalterne* (Rome: Coines, 1977).
Remy, Jean, "Innovations et développement des structures: Les problèmes que pose l'institutionalisation," *Lumen Vitae* (Brussels) 2 (1969): 201–28.
——, et al., "Formes religieuses en transformation: Rapport à l'ordre social et aux structures symboliques," in *Religion and Social Change,* Acts of the 13th Conference, Lloret de Mar (Lille: Secrétariat CISR, 1975), pp. 87–110.
Rey, Pierre-Philippe, *Las alianzas de clases* (Mexico City-Madrid-Buenos Aires: Siglo XXI, 1976).
Richard, Pablo, *Cristianos por el socialismo: Historia y Documentación* (Salamanca: Sígueme, 1976).

Romero, Rafael A., "Comentarios en torno a la obra *Marxismo y religión*," *Huella* (Los Teques, Venezuela) 3 (1977): 33 ff.
Scharf, Betty, *Sociological Study of Religions* (New York: Hutchinson, 1970).
Social Compass 24 (1977): 157-280 (on the tributary mode of production).
Sombart, Werner, *The Jews and Modern Capitalism* (London: Unwin, 1913); reprint (New York: B. Franklin, 1969).
Stavenhagen, Rodolfo, *Agrarian Problems and Peasant Movements in Latin America* (New York: Doubleday, 1970).
———, *Sept thèses erronées sur l'Amérique latine ou comment décoloniser les sciences humaines* (Paris: Anthropos, 1973).
Suaud, Charles, "L'école de la vocation," doctoral diss. (Paris: Ecole Pratique des Hautes Etudes, 1975).
Sunkel, Osvaldo, and Paz, Pedro, *El subdesarrollo latinoamericano y la teoría del desarrollo* (Madrid: Ed. Universitaria/Mexico City: Siglo XXI, 1973).
Touraine, Alain, *La conscience ouvrière* (Paris: Seuil, 1966).
———, *Production de la société* (Paris: Seuil, 1973).
———, *Pour la sociologie* (Paris: Seuil, 1974).
Vega-Centeno Bocangel, Imelda T., "Campo político—campo religioso—luchas populares y coyuntura en el Perú—Estudio de un conflicto laboral en al año 1971," licentiate diss. (Louvain: Institut des Sciences Politiques et Sociales/UCL, 1976).
Vidales, Raúl, and Kudo, Tokihiro, *Práctica religiosa y proyecto histórico: Hipótesis para un estudio de la religiosidad popular en América Latina* (Lima: CEP, 1975).
Weber, Max, *The Protestant Ethic and the Spirit of Capitalism* (New York: Scribner's, 1930).
———, *Economy and Society: An Outline of Interpretive Sociology*, Günther Roth and Claus Wittisch, eds., trans. E. Fischof et al. (Totawa, N.J.: Bedminster, 1968).
Wilson, Bryan, *Religious Sects: A Sociological Study* (New York: McGraw-Hill, 1970).

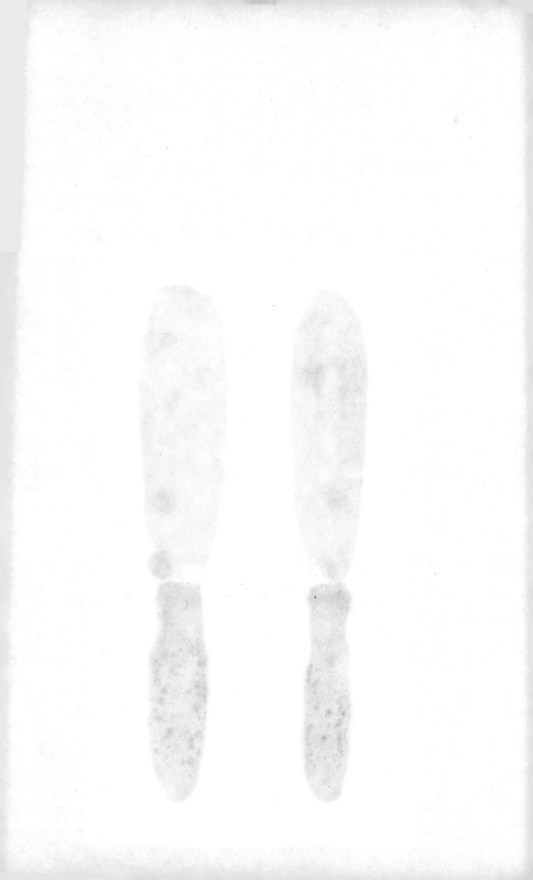